ELIZAMAE ROBINSON

SPEAKING Poetically

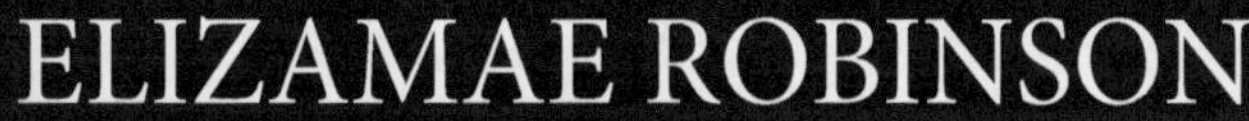

Elizamae Robinson
Speaking Poetically

ISBN: 978-1-947741-92-8

Published by Kingdom Publishing, LLC
1350 Blair Drive, Suite F, Odenton, MD 21113

Printed in the U.S.A.

Well, here it is folks.
My very own book. I never dreamed that I would be
writing poetry to the extent that I have. I have loved poetry
since my elementary school days and taking nothing for
granted. To God be the glory for the gift He has granted
me. I thank my children, grandchildren, church and
friends, from whom much of the inspiration came, that
allowed me to speak poetically.

Elizamae Robinson

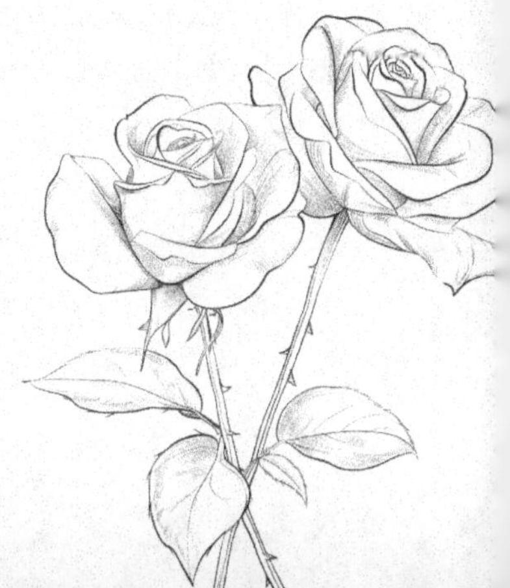

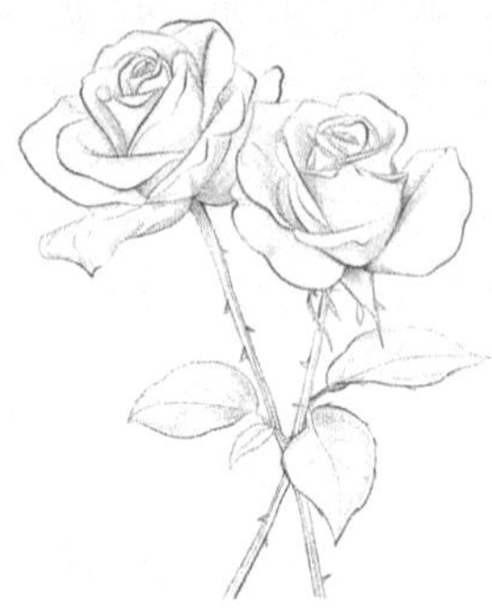

Our Destiny

There is a destiny we each have to face,
one our creator, our God put in place
from the very beginning when He knew our name,
He knew what would be gall us,
our joy, our pain.

As we come into the world so must we descend,
on a journey of life to a death, us our end.
Our encounters with others was all meant to be
the disasters awaiting us we all got to see.
The happiness, the good times was all part of the plan,
as well as the sadness and the mysteries for man.
For God put in place this destiny for man
with his full measure of love as part of the plan.

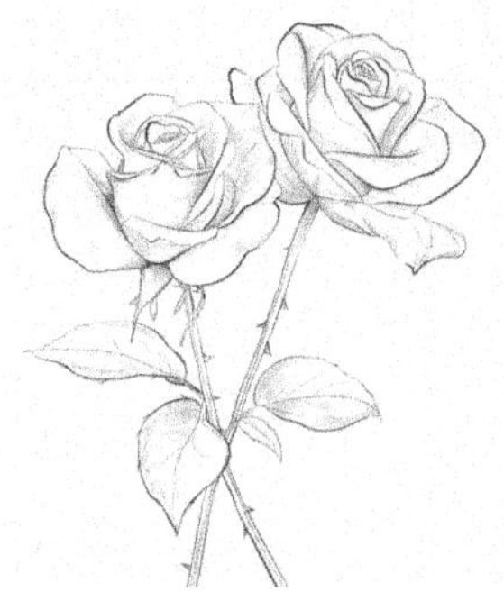

I Speak to You

I speak to you and said hello,
You asked me who I am
I said I'm here to help because
I see you're in a jam

I come in peace and offer love
I hope you'll do the same
It's time to do away with hate
That's part of Satan's game

We need to gird our strength
And cast him out
He causes pain and grief
He steals our pride and love of self
He's nothing but a thief

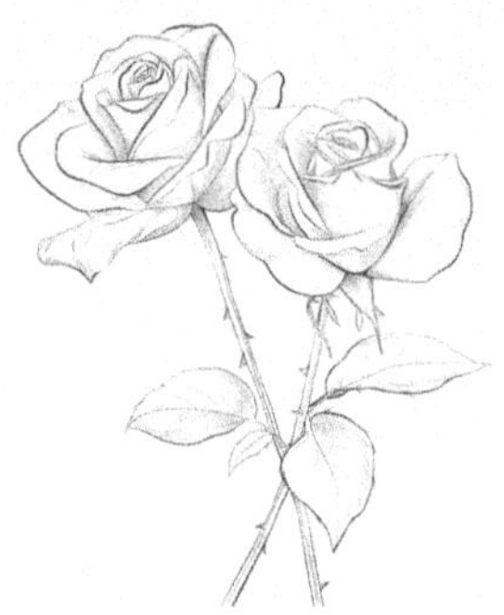

America Does Not Love Us

Black Americans love America
but does America love us?
I remember the days gone by
riding the back of the bus

White folks brought us here from
our African lands
they chained us, enslaved us
and made their demands

Those Saturday nights when police
beat up our brothers
showed no respect when approached
by our mothers
get back, they would say, or
we'll arrest you too
you people just don't know
what to do

Back then, when separate but
equal were the rules of the day,
black only, white only, were
the signs on display

We enriched America with slave
labor, music, science and art
America tried making us think
we weren't smart
Despite the hardships endured,
we remained Americans true

America Does Not Love Us

Justice, equality, even reparations
are long overdue, seemingly
So we will march and protest
and raise a bit of fuss
because America in part
has no love for us

All lives matter of course they do
and of course Black lives matter too
Killing Black men must cease
and so No Justice, No Peace

True we have come a long way
and we are not yet done
in the words of Martin Luther King Jr.
we shall overcome.

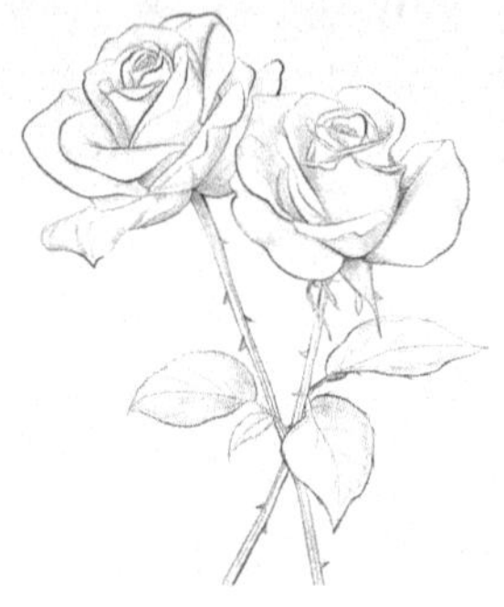

Come Together

Here we go, here we go, here
we go again,
marching in the streets for
our brother who was slain,
killed by the police who
kneed on his neck.

It's happening all too often.
Please give us a break.
black lives matter, just as
theirs do too.

All lives are made by God,
not just white and blue,
men must come together

Justice must prevail,
until it does, we all will
suffer rain, wild fires and hail.

Brothers killed by police must
come to a stand still
or God's fury will reign down
and purge the earth He will

Mankind made by God is
not man's to destroy.
The universe and all within
was made for God's own joy,
So watch out man, how you
Walk on the cross,
Your foot could slip and
Your soul will get lost

Stop the killing of black
Brothers in the street and
All lives come together,
for a soulful meet.

7

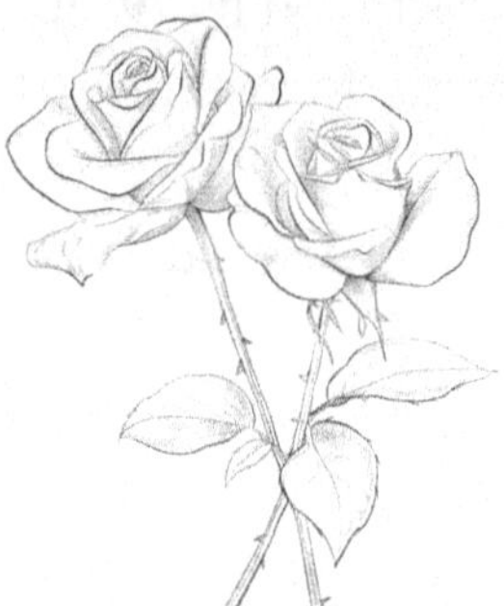

Please Stop The Killing

To my young and old beautiful black brothers,
This is one of your old black mothers
Speaking to you for so many others,
Please, stop the killing!

Don't you realize you're playing right in the hand
Doing just what's expected by the man
The one who is keeping your head in the sand,
Please, stop the killing!

Take time and think that at the end of the day,
All the brothers and sisters you've put out on the way,
Even killing the babies who will no longer play,
Please, stop the killing!

Don't always think it's about you or me,
We are a strong loving people together it's we,
So be the man, the man, the leader you were meant to be,
Please stop the killing!

The black family, need you to stick around,
To be the leader for which you were bound,
To lead, to love and to wear your kingly crown,
Please, Please, Please stop the killing!

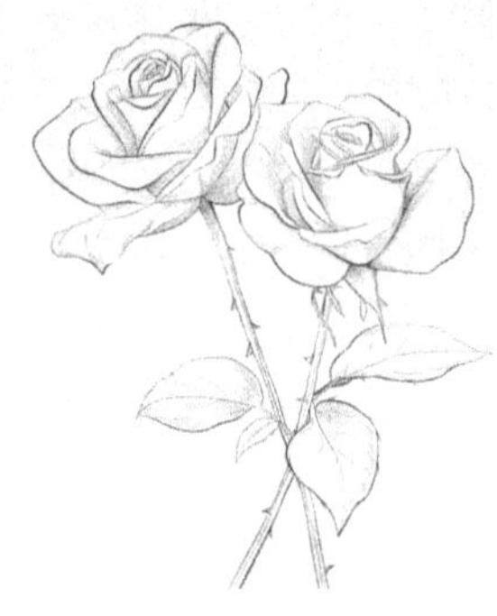

About Mildred

My daughter, my friend has gone onto glory.
She left behind a great legacy and wonderful story.
I did not expect her to go before me,
But I don't question God's will or what is to be.
She was placed in my care to serve on this earth.
God gave her life, I just gave her birth.
She fulfilled her destiny and God's plan for her,
Namely a mother, a care giver, as well as a teacher,
She weathered her storms and conquered her fear,
And seemed quite prepared as the end came near,
And finally life ended and she gave up the ghost,
And went home to glory where God is the host.

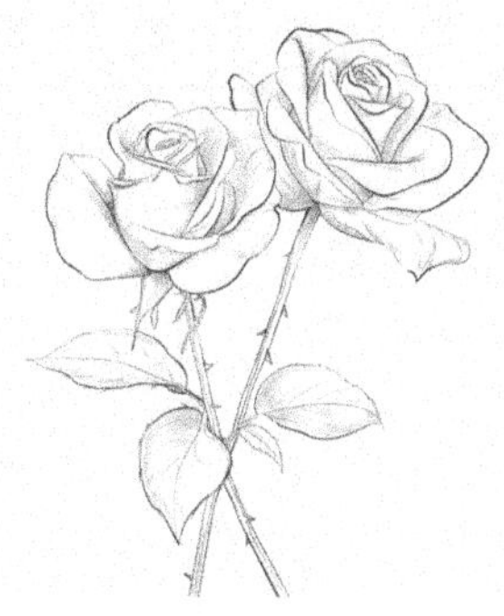

Jesus Is Waiting

Jesus is waiting for you to come home,
Walk away from sin you won't be alone
Others before you came home to the master
They picked up their cross and walked from disaster
You were blindly held captive by Satan the liar
But your father in Heaven was around to inspire
He never left you, His promise He kept
With arms out stretched He will welcome you
And said as He wept All along I was with you
You were never alone I'm still waiting my son
You'll be welcomed, come home.

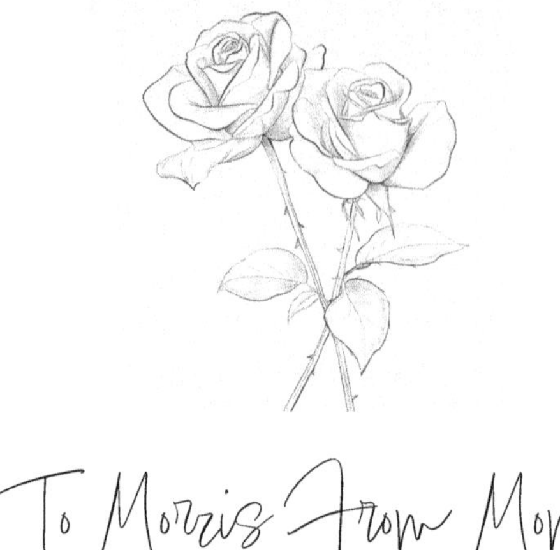

A Son, A Father, Brother, Uncle, Cousin and Friend
God brought you into this world,
And God took you out,
Without a lot of fanfare
Also without a shout.

He knew you were tired,
You were weary and so
He felt your pain and said to Himself
It's time for Morris to go.

He said, why keep you in a world that's dreary
Knowing you where tired and weary;
Your family loved you very much,
But we were glad God got in touch.

It was better for you to be with God the Master
Than in this world filled with disaster.
He has a place in his plan for you,
One, where you will have a better view.

So, you quietly left and went away
You knew you weren't here to stay
Your loving presence will always be near,
Though, you are no longer here.

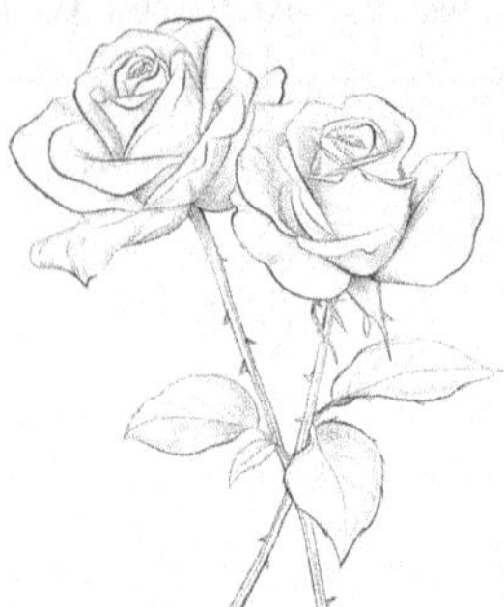

It Was Still A Good Year

Looking back at the year in retrospect,
Thinking about its cause and effect,
There were some joys and there was
Some fear,
With god in control
It was still a very good year.

We lost some friends and some
Family members too,
When we think of them, we fell
A little blue
Because to us they were oh so dear,
But with god in the mix, it was
Still a good year.

So to the year that's past and the
Year ahead of us,
Our thanks to god in whom we
Put our trust.
He gives us hope, peace and love
As he is always near

We can still look forward to
A very good year.

So happy new year to one and all.
Stay prayerful and mindful
To what may be your call,
Love everyone whether far or near,
And be thankful for another
God given year.

15

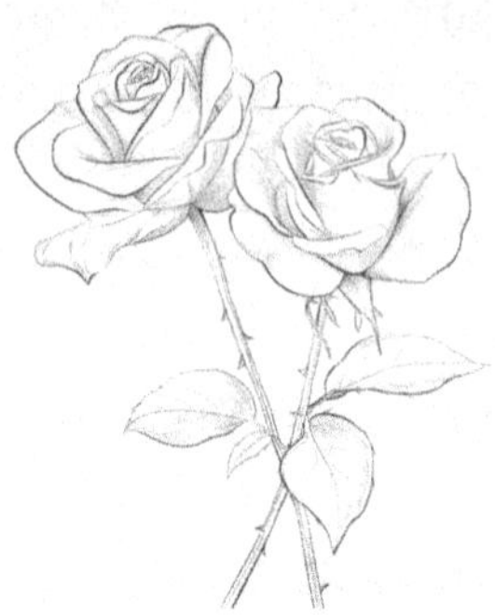

Especially for Jasmine

This poem is special because it tells
Of a loved one who thinks I'm swell'
But she is the one who is oh, so sweet
The things she does are extremely neat

She keeps in touch with all the others
The cousins, sisters, brothers and their mothers
I'm speaking of JASMINE, named after the flower
She is kind and thoughtful and loaded with power

The power of sweetness and plenty of love
Given to her by her father above
She's brilliant with smarts she's willing to share
She gives because she happens to care

She's dedicated to the students she teaches
Who happens to think she's all cream and peaches
She is all that and a bag of chips
With her love, encouragement and her handful of tips

She's her mother's child and her grandmothers delight
She's JASMINE for sure she's super sweet and super bright
She's loved by us all and we want her to know
She will always be the star of the show

17

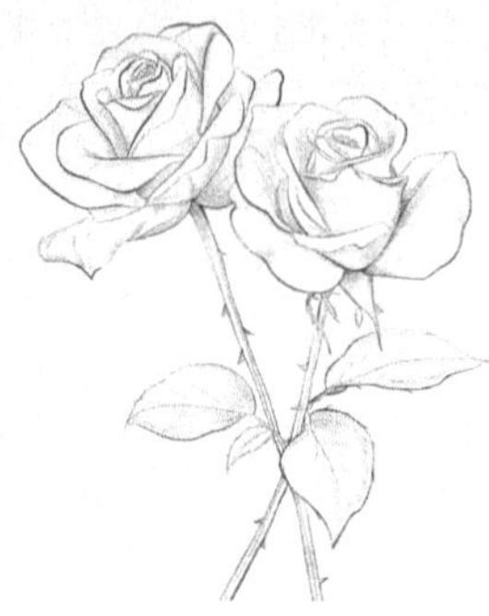

God's Gift To Mankind

God gave to mankind this vast
universe from sea to sea,
With deep valleys and high
mountains,
He gave for free.

Thousands of stars that light
Up the sky
Plenty of sunlight as each
Day go by

Trees filled with fruit that is
Good to eat
Flowers so beautiful,
Some red as a beet.

He gave man a woman
To have as his mate
They soon come together
To procreate

18

He gave children who run
Around, get together and play
He gave a time for work and rest,
At the end of the day.

Let us give thanks for a mind
That is open and clear,
Days, weeks and months that
Make up a year.
All this, God gave man time
After time
Each Christmas is His special
Time to shine.

So give to God what He is due,
The life, love and commitment
He gave each one of you.

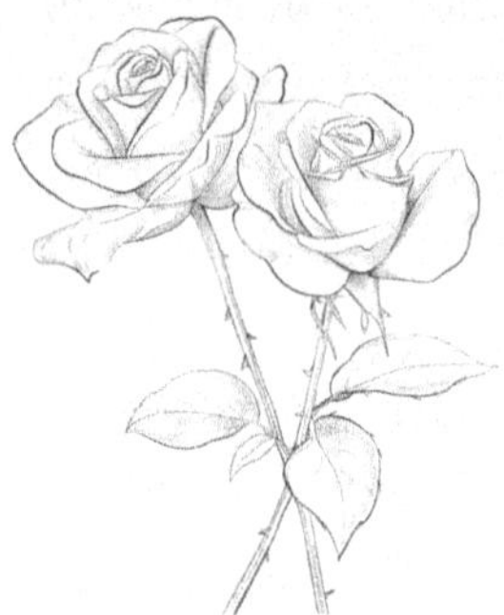

A Remembrance Of Friends

Whuttie, John Henry, Skeet and Beans,
The original good, bad boys,
Football, baseball and fighting,
Was always their games and their joys.

Growing up in the Fourth Ward
Playing ball on the back lot
The folks on Northwest, Clay and Calvert Streets
Knew those Boys were hot.

They were friends forever, always together
Thru the rain, thru the snow, or whatever.
Throughout the town they were all known well,
When tragedy struck and Beans was the first who fell.

Later on in life, good boy Skeet went on home to glory,
Leaving John Henry and Whuttie to finish out their life's
story,
John eventually left this earth and made his final great pass
To Whuttie who kept the legacy alive, now the good boys are
Together again At Last.

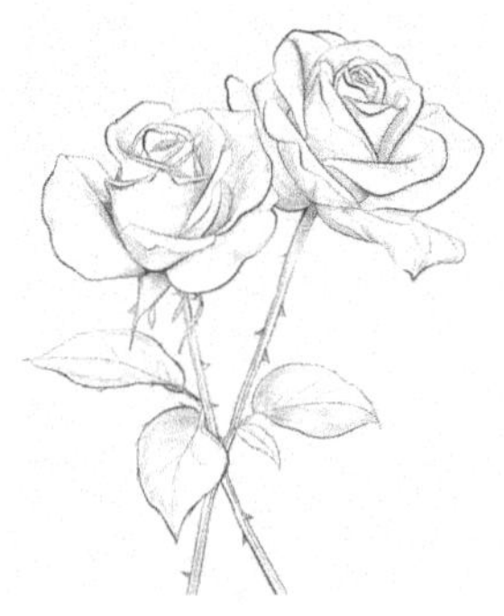

My Prayer, My Praise

Yesterday I thought about tomorrow
Which for me will be a day of joy, and not of sorrow
Tomorrow turned out to be today
A good day for me I must say
Because it's another milestone in my life
A life that has had its share of strife
It wasn't always easy, but I made it through
Thanks to my Savior and all of you
To be surrounded with family, friends and loved ones.
On my eightieth birthday, I've seen many moons, many
suns,
Days and nights far beyond what God promised me.
And I don't worry about what is to be.
His plan is already laid out for me, so I'll continue on until
life is through.
Grateful and thankful it was connected with you and you,
and you.
So thanks be to God until the end.
Thanks be to God, Amen.

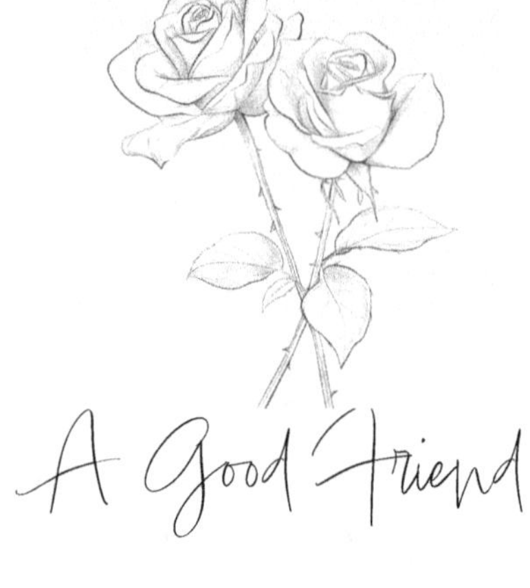

A Good Friend

Ain't it nice to have a friend
One on whom you can depend
Lifts you up when you are sad
Makes you smile and makes you glad
One who is always there for you
Around when things go wrong
And reminds you there's time to be strong
Takes you back to childhood days
Remembering then how kindness pays
All the things you did together
When sun was shining, even bad weather
When time seemed to be no end
Good times comes around the bend
But when it all comes to an end
I thank you God for my good friend
Everyone should have a friend
One on whom they can depend

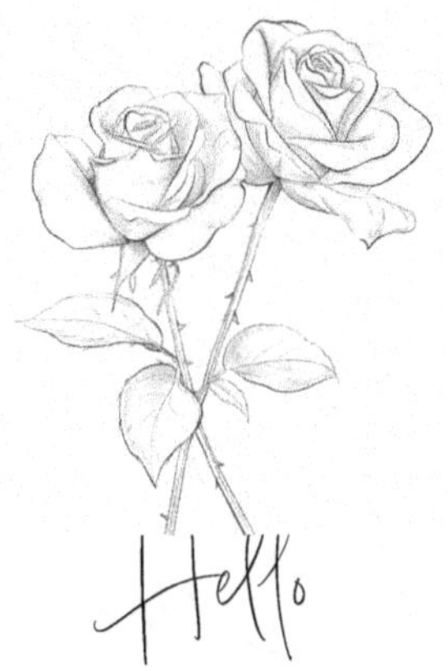

Hello, Hello, here's a note to say
We wish for you a very good day
To let you know we think of you
As a friend, we know is tried and true
A note we hope will bring a smile
And a whisper of love once in a while
We miss the look on your cheery face
And thoughts remain as you continue the race
The journey of life can be long
So keep the faith and remain strong
In the meantime our note's to say
Have a very, very good day

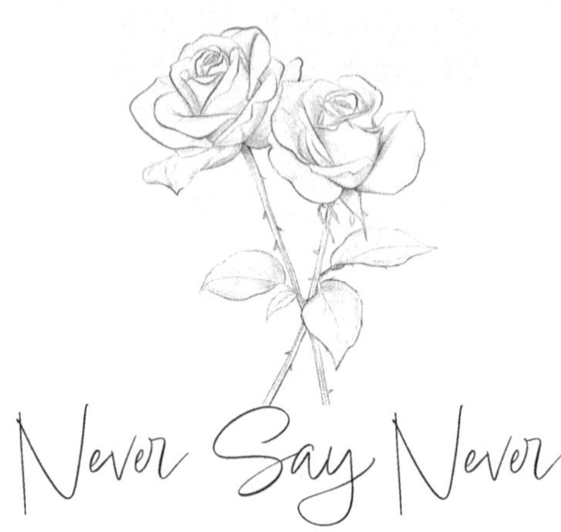

Never Say Never

Never, never say you won't
Never, never say you don't
Never say you won't and
Don't want to fall in love

Never, never say you will
Never, never say you still
Never, never say you will
Still never fall in love

So, if you ever do have
A change of mind
You might catch yourself a great friend
And find yourself falling in love

So, never, never, never
Ever, ever, ever say what you won't do;
Cause you may never, never, never,
Ever, know what's ahead for you.

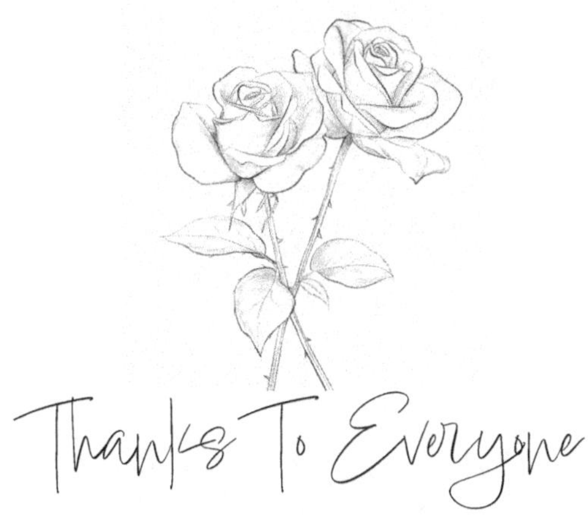

Thanks To Everyone

Thanks to you for being a friend,
You are one of the beautiful people,
You give help when folks need you,
With love as high as a steeple.

You give what you have to one and all
Always ready to serve from the moment they call.
No judgement or hesitation from you,
Just giving with love, is what you do.

God gives us friends on our journey thru life,
Could be classmates, a husband, or a wife.
What one they be, be thankful to thee
For sharing His love with you and me.

Whatever we give, we can't beat God's giving
If we follow His path as long as we're living.
He'll round us with friends to the very end,
Thank you, to everyone who is my friend.

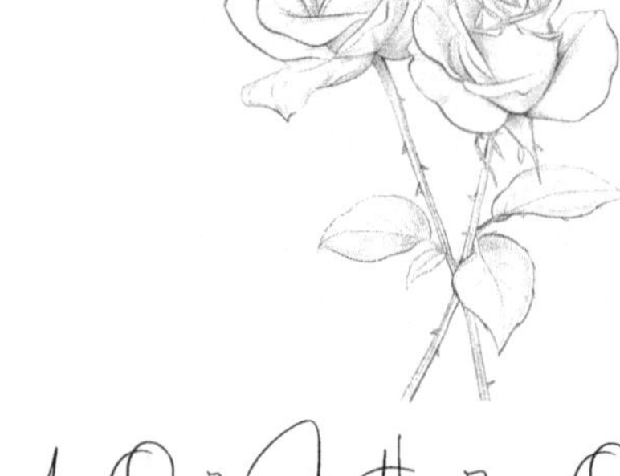

God Our Father, Our Mother

From generation to generation
We are many, but one nation
Under the sun
Made possible from the One,
I am your sister
You are my brother
All of us related to one another
Down thru the ages we came many strong,
Marching thru time, turmoil and trouble bringing
Each along
Creating families from shore to shore
Enlarging the nation more and more
And as we move on one thing can be said
To each born and each other
We love you God, My Father, My Mother
Who cared for and nurtured me and my brother,
Who was there with us through the night
And stayed with us til the break of light
You fed us and led us and kept us safe
Till this day

We love thee so much, what more can we say
Almighty, dear God, our Father is He who made
All things, all things meant to be
He brought into being even Jesus our brother, God,
Dear God, our Father, our Mother
The promise was given, the prediction came true
Just as He said it would and all right on cue.

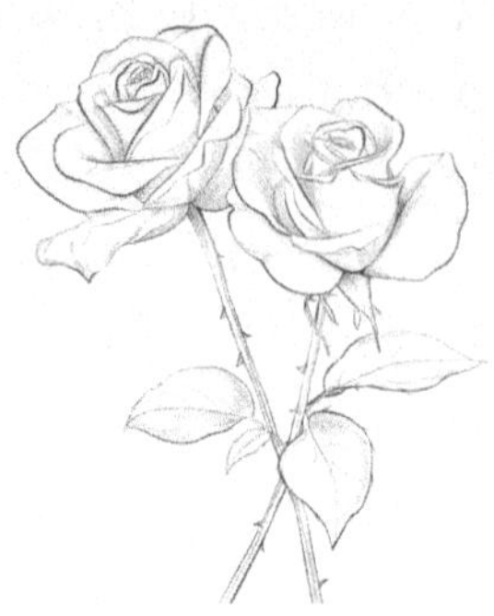

Old Folks

Let's tell a story about
Our folks of old,
About the lives they lived,
Their stories untold,
Of the babies out of love
That was born.
And the ones that came
Amid lots of storm
The dreams our folks had
That never came true
Their hope for tomorrow that
Was long overdue
Their church in the woods
That kept hope alive
In spite of their kin folk that
Was strung up and died.
Many days they spent full of joy
Because they had love for
Some little boy,
Or a little girl full of laughter as

She ran in the sun,
Or as folk came together when
Days work was done,
There are many stories and
Much yet to be told.
Of our brave black Americans
And those days of old.
The future of families as they
Came down the lines

The contributions they made
That was ever so fine.
To make life so much better was
Always their aim,
And we of today, can attest to that claim.
When I speak of my ancestors
Those dear folks of old.
Despite the fact that as slaves
They were sold.
Dear Lord, I shout out ever so loud
Dear Lord, I thank you, I'm black
And I'm proud.

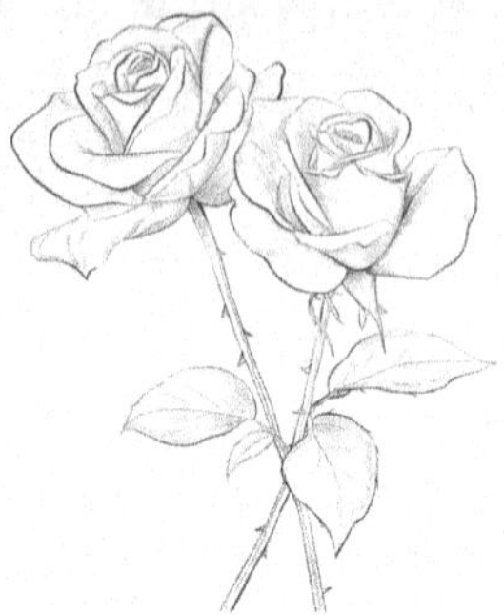

To: Mr. and Mrs. Tinker

Tinker, Tinker Little Star

Tinker, Tinker shining star,
Can't help wonder how you are,
Quite the gentle folks by far,
Guided by God's greatest star.

Stars above the sky so bright,
Helps me keep your smile in sight.
Stay the course and run the race,
Sit quietly in your special place.

Converse with God, who loves you so,
More than you ever know.
So keep your stars shining bright,
To light your smile every night.

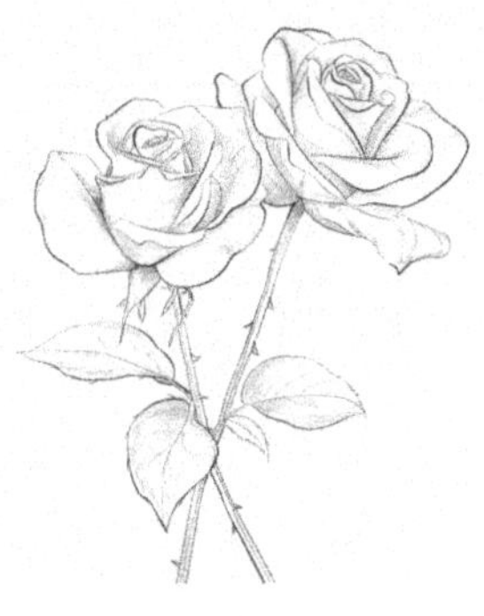

Someday

Someday and by God's grace,
There won't be several, be one race,
Only one nation under one sun
When the battle with Satan is
Finally won,
But, until that happens folks had
Better take heed,
And stop all this hating, and
Be a better breed.
Start living a life that's filled with love.
If you wish to join loved ones
In heaven above
Start treating your fellow man with respect,
You'll be amazed how that will affect.
What a change and turn around it will bring about,
A better relationship without a doubt.
So start today, say you'll begin,
To be a better person, determined to win,
Favor with God who resides up above,
You'll reap your reward because you chose to love.

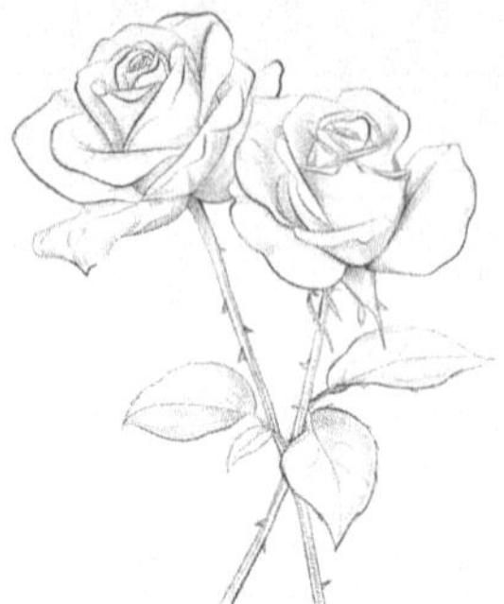

Today, Love Somebody

Love somebody
Hug somebody today,
Greet somebody and
Shake a hand today,
Be kind and loving
Do some hugging today,
Send some flowers
To someone you love today,
Wave a hand and smile
At someone today,
Give a shout out, run
And jump about today,
It's not too late to
Forgive somebody today,
You'll feel much better
After loving somebody today,
Tell somebody that
God is love today,
And yell out, I love, love,
Love you today, always.

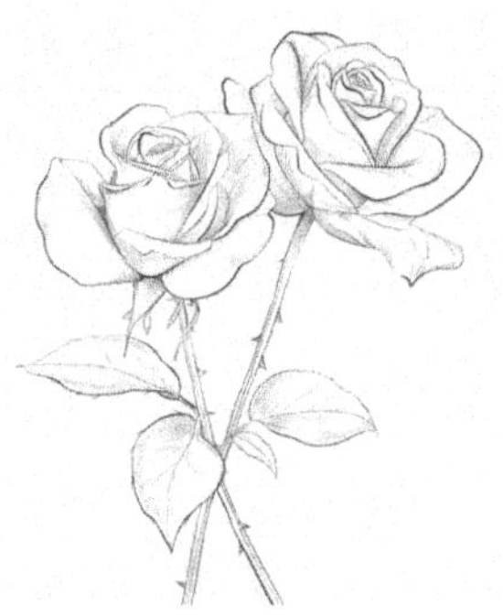

We Are Where He Wants Us To Be

We talk, we fuss and we complain,
And every bit is done in vain,
Because, whatever our lot in life you see
Is exactly where God wants us to be.

He puts us to sleep at night,
And wakes us to the morning light,
Gave us another day set free,
Exactly where God wants us to be.

He sends us out along our way
To work or just to spend the day,
To live with love is the key
And exactly where God wants us to be.

He listens to us, He holds the line,
He answers our prayers all in His time,
While in control of land and sea,
We, His children are always where He
Wants us to be.

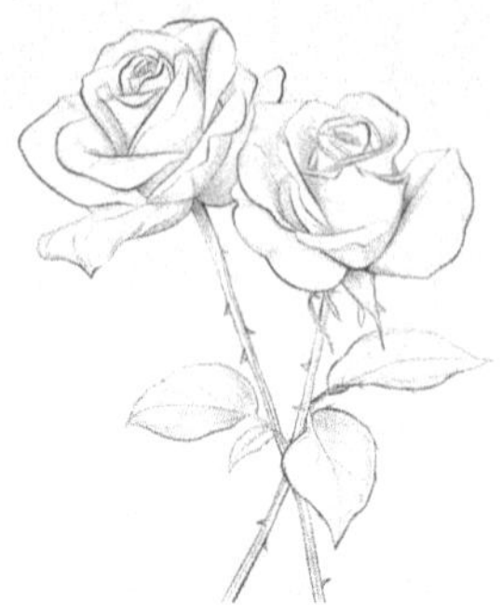

Rendering

If you owe Ceasar listen to what I say,
One way or another he will make you pay,
You'll give what you owe much to your sorrow,
If not today, you will tomorrow,
If not by then, years later he'll come,
Believe me by then he will have doubled the sum,
You don't get away, you'll pay what you owe,
You'll lose your car, your house, or your dough.
You can not cheat the government and think you can win,
To not pay what you owe is the ultimate sin,
So take my advice and pay off your debt,
You'll feel a lot better, maybe have something left.
It's hard but its fair, give the tax man his due.
After taking what is his, he'll give the rest to you.

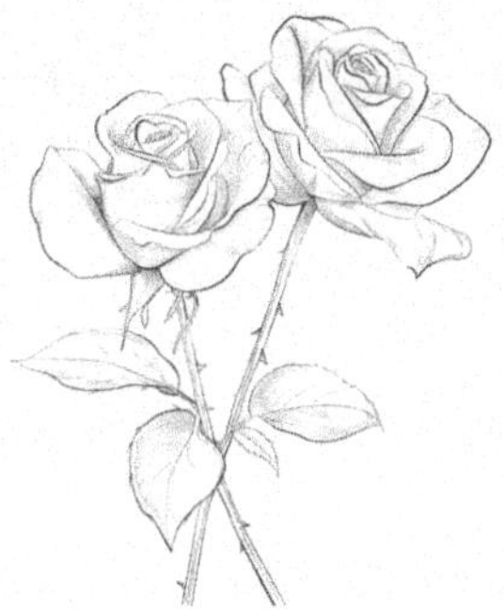

We Who Are Born

We who are born and have yet to die,
Can thank our Lord who reigns on high,
Sometimes we are led to know
When it is our time to go,
Yet we live on until that time,
The lovely, the lonely, the sublime,
We live on until our task is at end,
When He alone takes us around the bend,
So until then we keep living, keep loving,
Our own,
Keep giving the praise to Him alone,
Keeping the youth until He gives
Us the call,
It is then we can say our good bye
To all

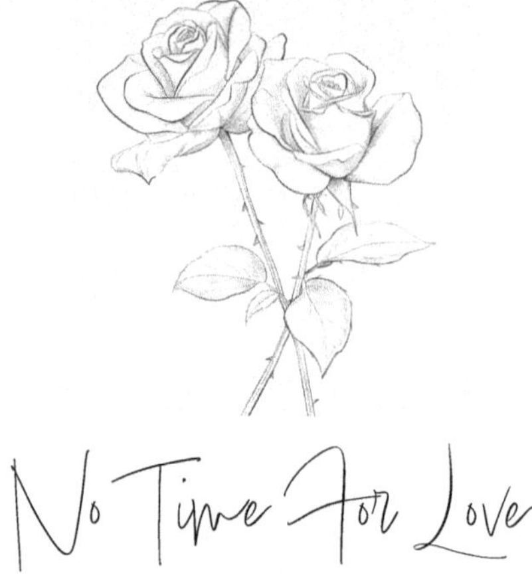

No Time For Love

Time is quickly slipping away,
No hellos' or goodbyes'
During the day
No thoughts of me has been
On your mind,
No calls to say how are you dear,
No visits yet far or near
Yet time is quickly going by
Still no hellos' or friendly his'
But that's okay, cause my
Thoughts of you
Have all been happy never blue,
I will continue to think of you
That way
When evening is nigh and
At the end of the day,
I will love you still.

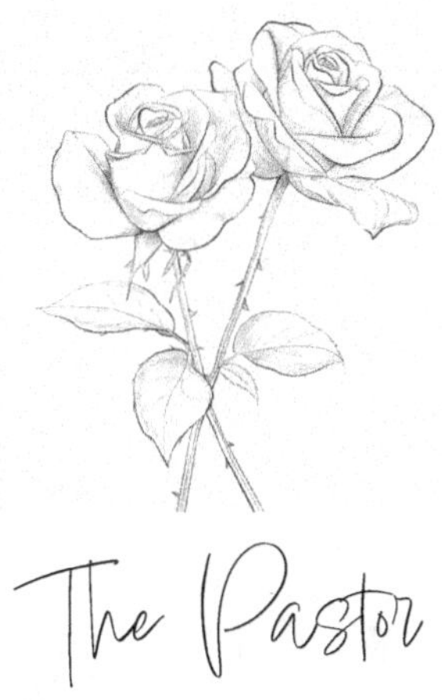

The Pastor

The Pastor is the earthly Shepherd of God's flock
The Pastor for the most part is as solid as a rock
Our own Pastor Boston is really quite a gem,
A most generous and honorable man found among men.

He has served God and his country which is quite a task
All with great honor, what more can we ask
He has given sixteen years of service to First Baptist as well,
And to this fine city he has also been swell.

He has continued the legacy of Pastors before him,
Developing Boston Commons has been quite a win,
Hail to the chief who was sent from up above,
Sent to us from God himself with a lot of love.

This is from your congregation, who has this to say,
Sit back, relax, and enjoy yourself on your Anniversary Day
To God, family and country you have been quite awesome,
And we thank God for you, our own Pastor Boston

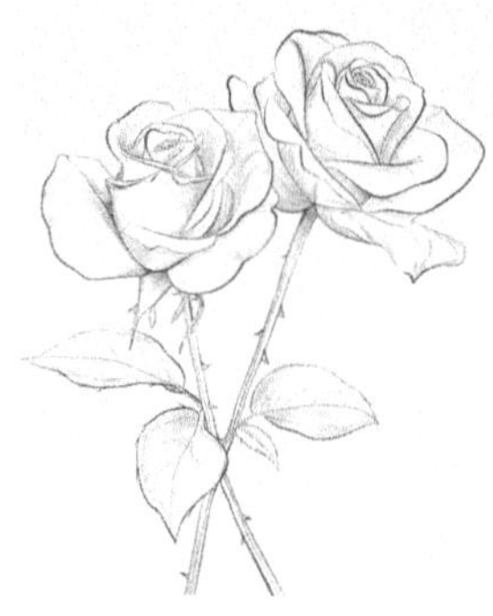

The Old Fourth Ward

No, no, no the old Fourth Ward
Is not what it used to be many long years ago,
We had our own of everything
White folks had and more,
We had our barber shops beauty shops and a
Store on old Spa Road.
And for a night out on the
Old town ward, we'd shift
To night club mode.
We had Washington Hotel, Wrights Hotel,
Cozy Cabin, and Susie's Tea Room man,
We had much fun in all these
Spots and everything was grand,
The American Legion and the
Elks Club, two private spots,
We did not have all we should've
But we had a lot.
Our churches spread across the town,
Our people served God well.
With Sunday School, Bible studies and

Church services were swell,
So, we don't forget from whence
We've come.
It's been a long, long way,
All praises due to God,
from then until today.

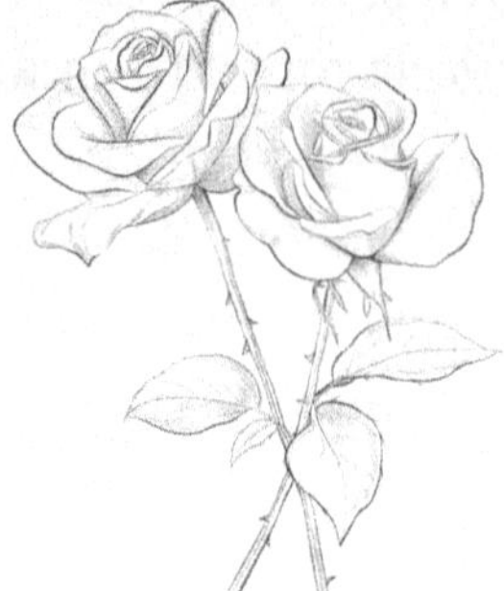

Up, Up and Away

I have gone beyond
Where the birds fly,
I have entered a higher
Portion of the sky,
I have passed the clouds,
That higher still,
Up to the gates on
Heaven's Hill
I passed some friends
On the way up,
We smiled, rejoiced and
We took of the cup,
They wished me well and
Said I'd meet,
Lots of relatives who I
Will get to greet,
I'm on my way to the
Heavenly Seat,
Since I have accomplished
Quite a feat,
I kept the faith
And served God well,

And now it's my turn
To ring the Heavenly bell,
So, stay true to your God,
Show plenty of love,
Until it's your time to
Come up above,
Who knows, you never
Can tell,
When you get to ring
Cont. Up, Up and Away

That Heavenly Bell.

41

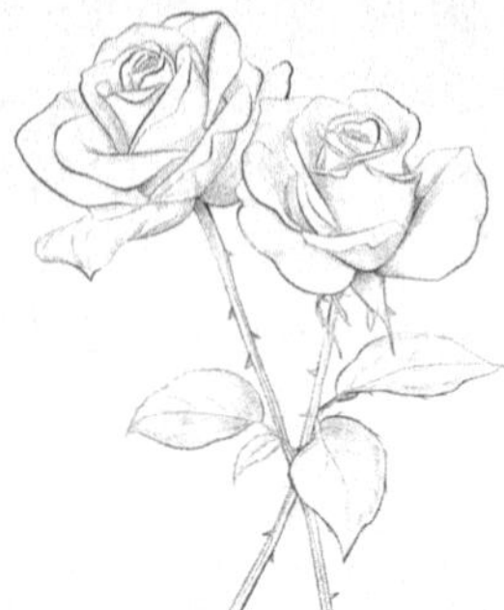

I'm Part of The Master Plan

As I increase my time in age,
I'm facing issues at this stage
I'm part of the Masters plan.

I may be going down, but I'm
Not out
I still have time for a little
More shout
As part of the Masters plan

I'm hangin on and staying strong,
Doing all that's right and
Nothing wrong,
Still part of the Masters plan

Love is the answer still, and yet
There is time to give and time to
Get,
I'm part of the Masters plan

I'm keeping the faith and walking
Hand and hand,

Staying connected to that
Awesome Man,
All part of the Masters plan

When my time is over and I
Answer His call,
Don't worry, I'll be at that
Heavenly Hall, I'm part of the Masters plan.
I call out your name

Years ago, we started out together
We went thru many storms
As well as good weather,
So, when you think of me
Call my name,
When I think of you I will do the same.
We somehow got thru times
That we're tough
Struggling thru life got really rough.
A lot of rough times were
Hiding around the bend,
And though we weren't together
At the end
I still think about you
And call your name.
You have gone on and can't do the same.

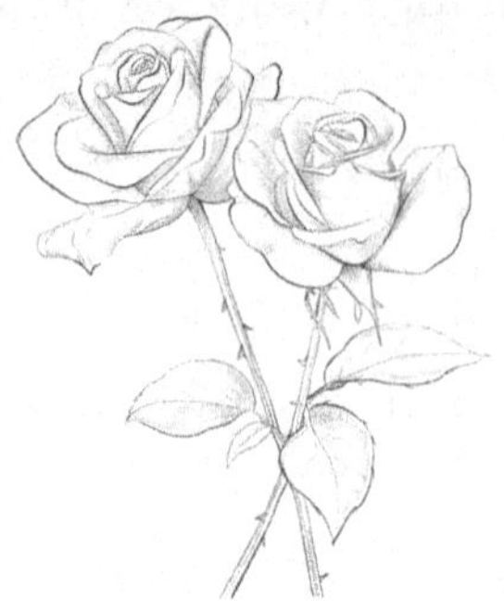

He is in Control

After dinner when we have been fed,
When not much later we go off to bed,
Later still when we drift off to sleep,
And travel into a twilight deep,
Somewhere off into space to a place unknown
Maybe even to God's gracious throne
Gone somewhere in the dark of night,
We later return at the break of light,
Thank God we awaken to a bright new day,
Our thanks to God whose grace was at play
Always He is in control.
Continuously blessing our very soul,
Throughout the day we are in His keep,
Safe with the shepherd who watches
His sheep.

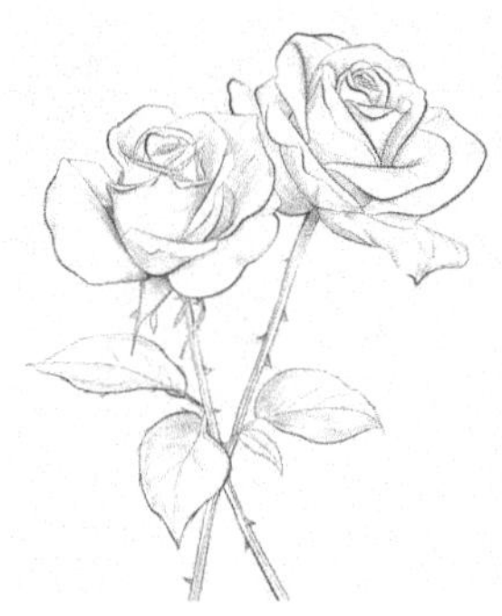

Use Your Voice

Change is not coming, it's already here
The Black community is losing all that is dear
Young men fighting, killing each other over drugs
Older folks dying now; maybe from some bugs
There's a virus that's killing folks all across
The nation
Mostly black folks, is of course
The sensation
Our schools are closed and so is the church
And we apparently are left in the lurch
But, your kids kept right on killing
And it is such a shame
You gambled on life and you lost the game
You could have been great but you made the
Wrong choice, still all is not lost if you just
Use your voice
To help others avoid making a mistake
Let them know there's a better road to take
If you settle disputes in a different way
You'll live a better life each and every day.

45

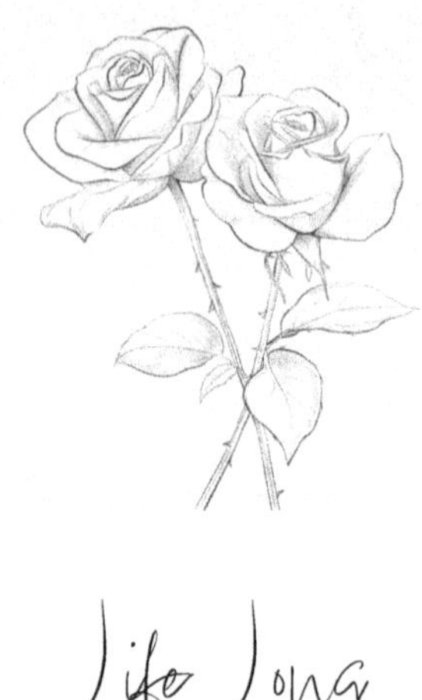

Life Long

God our father, creator of the earth and all that dwell therein,
The father who loves, protects us and forgives us when we sin
Whatever happens whether good or bad it's He it's all about
So we should always keep the faith and never fear nor doubt
We owe Him love and diligence in everything we do
With our heart and soul return to Him the love He gave to you
Love your neighbor as yourself and do no one any wrong
Keep His commandments from day to day, your reward could be
life long.

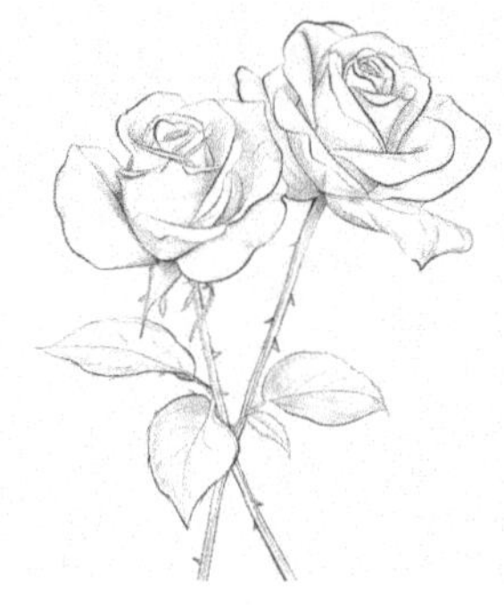

About Death

Death is not your enemy death will come to set you free
Set you free from the world's fares
Set you free from Satan's snares

God said man will surely die
You can't escape it if you try
Resign yourself that it will be your debt to pay to be sin free

Accept the Christ as our Lord and Savior
And death as our Lord's praise and favor
And death will come when it's your turn
You will claim the peace and grace you earn

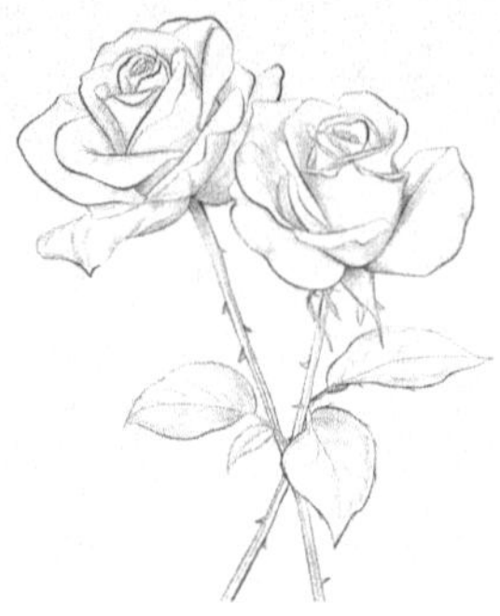

The Test

Around midnight when the T.V. is off and the lights are out
When you have settled down and stopped stirring about
Think about the day and how it was spent
How fast it came and how fast it went
Did you take the time to do a good deed
Spread a little love, help someone in need?
No! If you wake up the next morning you hit the road,
go west,
And thank God for another chance, He gave you to take
the test.

48

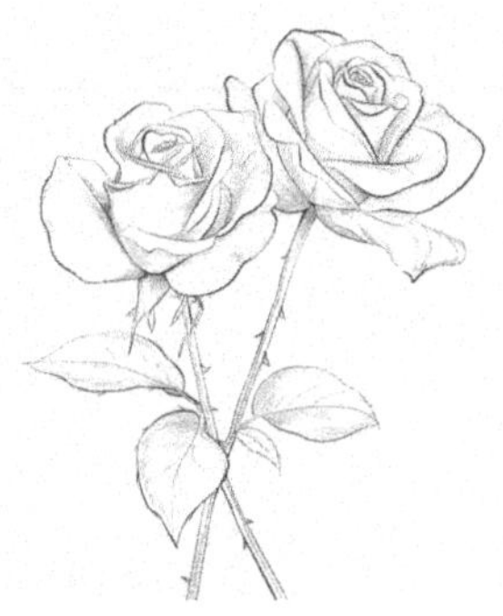

You Make the Choices

Once a body enters this world it's already,
really on its way out
God sets the time it is to remain and also sets the route
Life's journey starts, your purpose begins,
You may do some good, you may do some sins,
You make your choices, you pay your price
For the choices you keep or what you sacrifice,
You only get one chance, one chance at living.
Use it wisely, use it for giving.
The choices we make, good or bad
There are things we didn't do, but wish we had.
Anyway, death has a way of making you think.
Life can leave you in a nod or blink.
So do some good before you leave this earth
If you want to make it to the second birth.

49

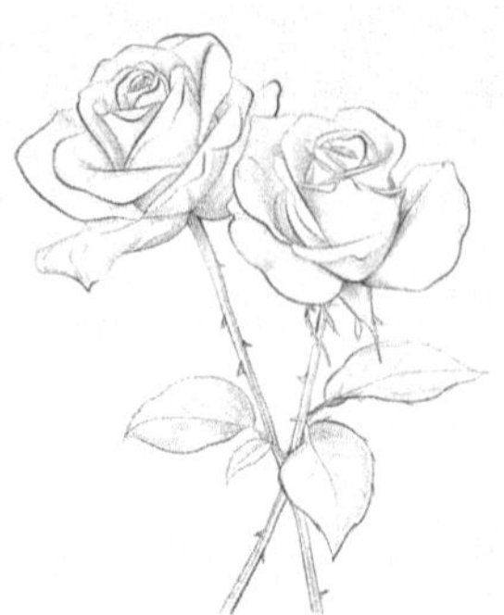

Women Walking In The Light Of the Holy Spirit

Women walking in the light of the Holy Spirit,
Silently walking by day and by night,
Women walking, doing God's will,
Walking tall and upright.

How great Thou art who took the earth of the land,
Made woman to be the mother of man,
Beautiful women having God's attributes,
Having intelligence and love no one can dispute.

Dutiful women working in the vineyards,
Patiently bringing in the sheep,
Assuring the men and women they will be in God's keep
Strong women holding down the fort
In truth and sincerity, with love and support.

Strong women who knew that they were sent,
To be loving, obedient and benevolent
The greatest gift God gave from the earth of the land,
Women walking in the light of the Holy Spirit which
He gave also to man.

50

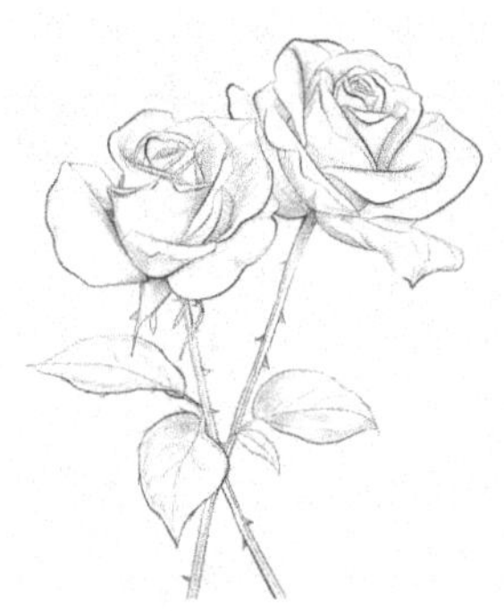

Men Of God

Jesus the son of God was the greatest man to ever live.
And God brought forth many great men who have so much
to give.
The nature of men is to resonate love. Their greatest gift
from God
above, men who can be as strong as an elephant or as gentle
as a bird,
men constantly seeking to understand God's word, men
faithful and loving to their wives, maintaining a way of life
that's sure to survive.
Making sure the children are reared with love for their
brothers. And making sure they never forget to show respect
for their mother. Men
who are strong, majestic and fearless, faithful loving men.
Sterling and
peerless men are kings and generals, bright shining stars,
brilliant
servers of God, that's what they are. What more can be said
about men
true til this day. Except true to themselves and to God they
will stay.

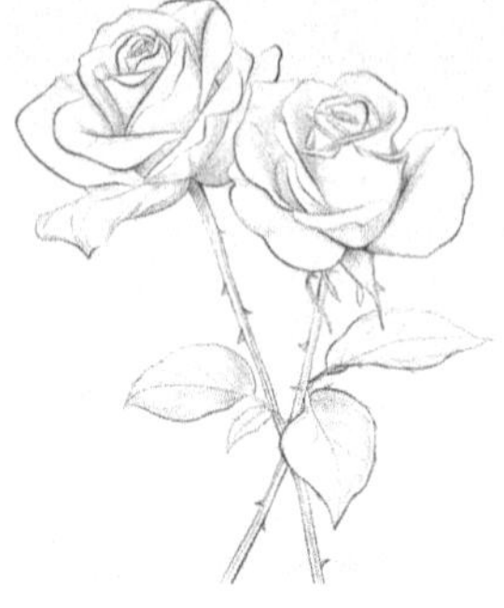

Bible Study

Listen everyone and all, and when you have heard,
heed this call.
Come to bible study on Saturday
and learn to live life God's way.

Friends gather at First Baptist Church, where they pray for
the sick before starting their search, of scriptures that gives
them God's word.
The likes of which, they have never heard.

They gain knowledge that helps them to know,
they share a love that helps them to grow.

God wants everyone to win, a life of love that's free from sin.
Some come out and bring a friend, who might be broken
and want to mend

They will gain a new life and lease, after receiving God's
sweet peace.

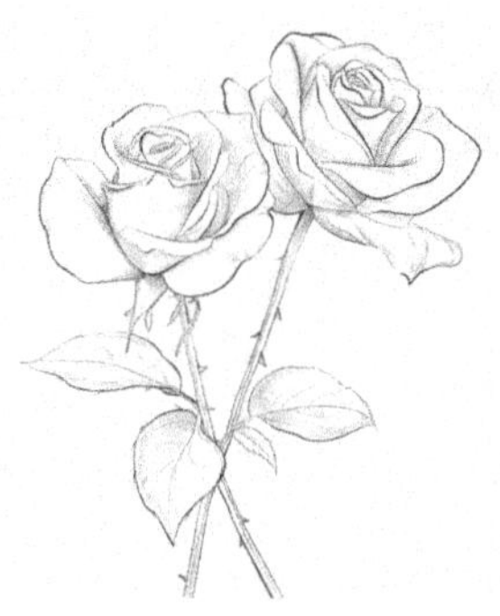

Growing Old

Growing old is no laughing matter,
you no longer hear the pitter and pater.
Of the children's feet as they run down the hall.
They are no longer to hear when you call.

They don't run up and down the stairs anymore.
There is no one there, no one slams the door.
So what's with the moms when kids are no longer there.
Are you left wondering if they even care?
Grandchildren also seem to forget about the past,
will they, fill the void of your children at last.

But feel no despair, they are just giving you space
to get back into life and keep up the pace
that you left behind when you had to face the task before
you, growing up and growing old.

Now that it's over, get back in the fold, life is not over just
because you're growing old.

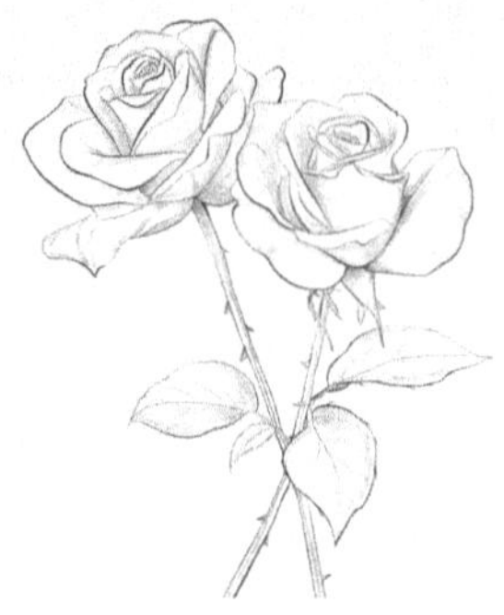

My Father

54

Black was the color of my father's skin, a personable,
charming man from within. His heart was as pure as the
first fallen snow, greeted always with love and respect as
he traveled to and fro. To his wife and his children he was
worth more than gold. When he spoke his voice was warm,
gentle, but bold. Never a more beloved man than he...
A man who was all about family. I'll remember him always,
with love in my heart, and thank the creator for giving him
his start.
To be the son of a great black father and as a sweet young
boy, to live a God given well lived life full of joy.

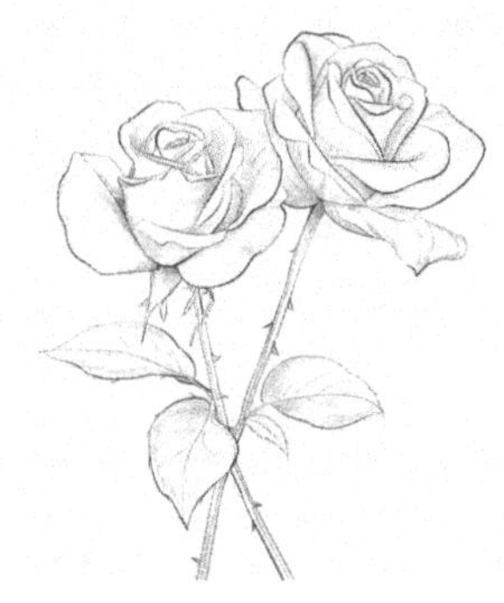

Stop the Hate

Let us come together and serve the Lord and stop venting so
much hate. You never know when your time is up stop now
before it's too late.

Don't be so small and not do what you could, be the bigger
person, stop the hate, because you know you should.

Watch out for Satan whose only deed is really to destroy, the
family that belong to God, every girl and boy on God we
stand.

God is love, He endowed us with love so we should love each
other. We are all for one and one for all, each sister and each
brother.

On God we stand a united front is where we all should be,
every other sister brother and that includes you and me.

55

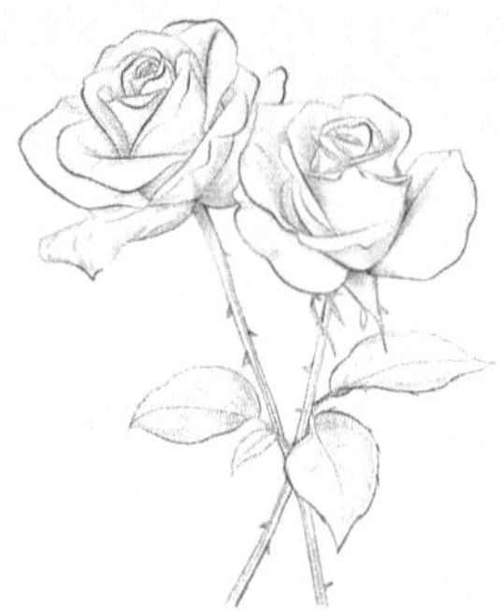

Speaking Poetically

The poems you read throughout these pages are things I
thought about thru various stages,
The words and thoughts are really me, and I'm speaking
poetically.

Annapolis is the city where I was born, and while I could, I
will not scorn, the racist treatment my people bared, I speak
the truth because I was there.

My God given gift of longevity, and the words that I speak
poetically, the words that I speak are not lightly taken, are as
true as my God whom I have not forsaken.

Treatment that I dare say from colonial times to this very
day, but no hateful feelings will there be, cause I'm living my
life abundantly.

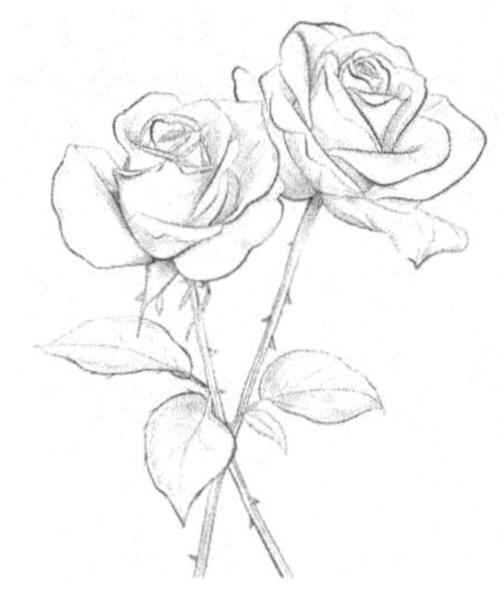

Only You Lord

My Lord, there is none like you in all the earth or on high.
You put the wet in water Lord and the blue in the sky.
You give us sunshine Lord on any given day.
You can make it rain dear Lord or take it all away.
You hung the rainbow in the air as a signal of your loving
care.
You heal our pain dear Lord and comfort us from sorrow.
You give us hope dear Lord for a brighter day tomorrow.
Yet on any given day Lord our flesh will turn to dust.
But the spirit and the love you give will never rot or rust.
So come what might or may dear Lord, until the very end.
We have you to thank dear Lord for all the joy you send.

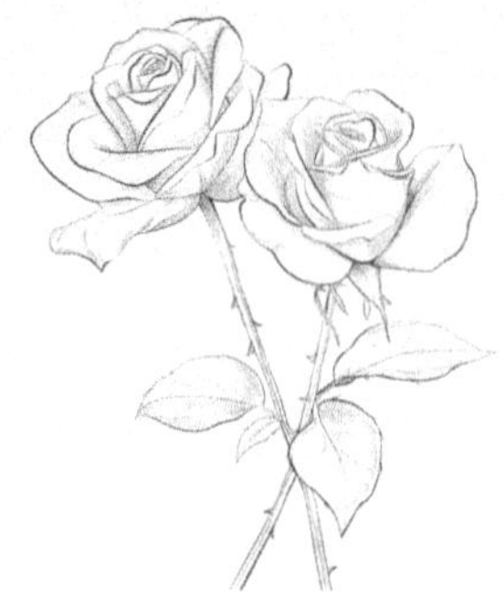

Wes is running for Governor and he is just the man, to lead this great state of Maryland.

Wes is one more black man coming up the ranks, many came before him, all giving God thanks.

For the opportunity to serve God, country and man, to show his love of Maryland and to lend a helping hand.

Trust him, support him, he'll leave no one behind, moving Maryland forward is what he has in mind.

Your vote for Wes can help him on his way, if you cast your vote for him on election, day.

With you behind him, he'll be sure to score.

So, come out, cast your vote for our own Wesley Moore.

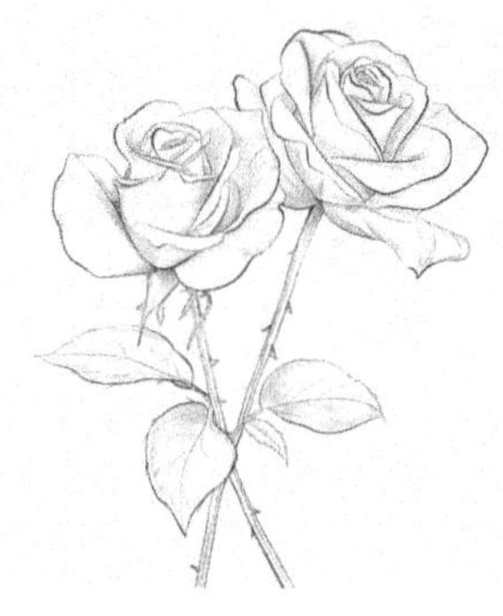

Oh, Maryland, dear Maryland I know a guy who is simply great.

He is next in line to lead this fascinating state.

He is wonderful and simply the best.

I'm talking about the guy named Wes.

He's a people person who will get what's due, for each and every one of you.

Great plans for Maryland he has in store.

Remember in November to vote for Wesley Moore.

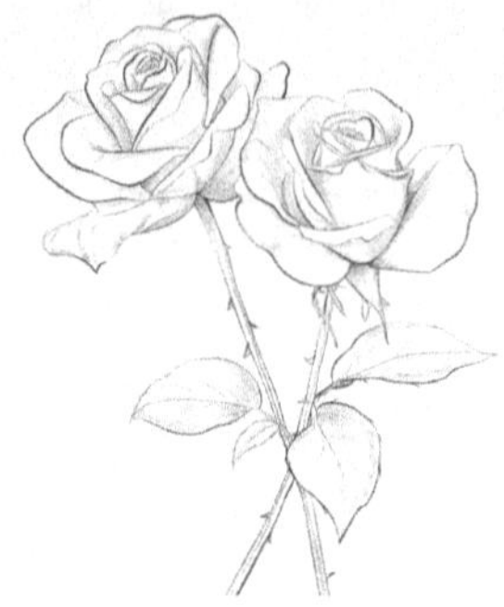

What the World Needs Now Is Love Sweet Love

...and more than you can imagine, because right now the tempest is raging. A lot of furious commotion is going on in our homes and in the streets all over this nation. So much violence, turmoil and agitation is taking place and our lives, for many of us, is in an uproar. Turmoil, violence and agitation are all words that Webster's dictionary describes as tempest Satan, the author of lies, keeps things in an uproar and constant chaos. Someone once said, "When you let Satan in your house you can't tell him what to do." Have we reached a point where we no longer rule over our household? If that is the case, the only thing we can look forward to is self-destruction and breakdown in true family values. If we believe there is a destructive force weaving their way in our lives we must also believe the opposite. A positive force that rules with truth, peace and love. Who can turn our lives around but the one and only creator, a higher power, even greater than Satan? No one that I know of because there is only one. So let's take advantage of the great overwhelming love that is at our disposal and use it to clean up our lives and our streets by passing it on; at least give it a try.

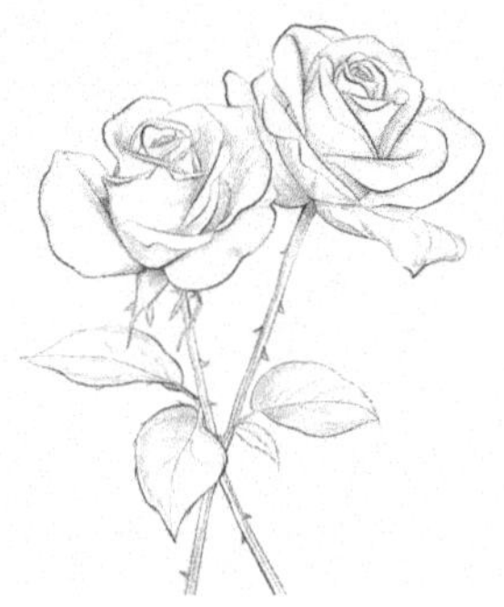

To the Sistahs and Brother Man

This is a reminder for all of us,
Who remember riding the back of the bus,
Well times have changed and so have we,
Thanks to Fannie Lou, Martin and Malcolm those amazing
three,
Along with many others who was a float,
Others who wasn't afraid to rock the boat,
They appealed to the masses and we all took note,
We took to the grapevine and got out the vote,
The call is going out once more,
To reach out, go out and knock on every door.
We can't afford to lose our gains,
To that bad movement going across the plains,
The sistahs and brothers must be made awake,
Democracy as we know it, is at stake,
So call out the troops, rally the folks once again to promote,
All the sistahs and brothers, who got out the vote.

61

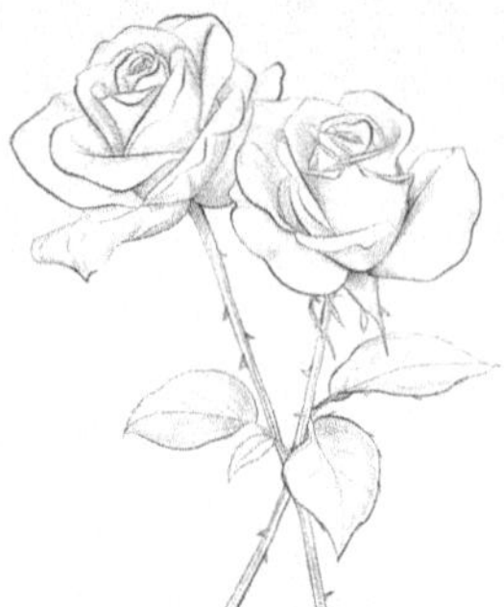

God Knows All About You

You are God's creation, so
He knows all about you.

And everything that happens to
You all happens right on cue.

Your yesterdays, today and
Your tomorrows, He brings them all about.

All your travels here and there
God puts on a certain route.

Everything you do in life
Believe me, He is aware.

He keeps a daily tab on you
All because he cares.

Because He loves you so
You are very high in ranks.

And every day that you have life
You should give Him praise and thanks.

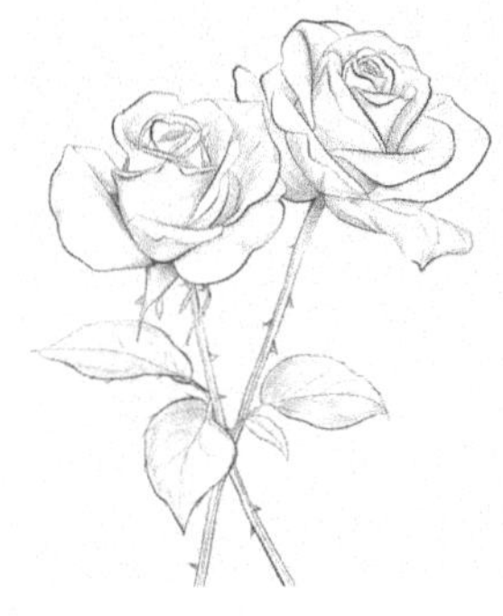

The Forward

Today is Family Day and I am here to talk about family and what it means to us. Family is the greatest institution in the world today created by God himself, and today we have come together to celebrate the ongoing of our Senior members of the family and our young people.

It is important that we continue to celebrate our reason for staying together. To pass on the baton to the younger people the love that has kept us going for generations. We have lost members of the family some old and some young, but we keep the connection between those of us still living. We were left a legacy of love and love is the connection.

So I pass onto you this poem written by a connected family member and its entitled the Love Connection.

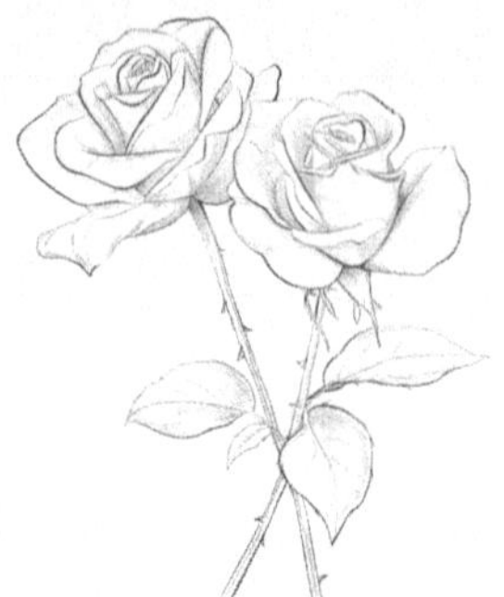

The Love Connection

Family was created by God for his pleasure,
God who is love himself by any measure,
Family is the existence of God's human tree,
Planted for his enjoyment we can agree,
He planted trees of green in His garden of forestry,
And trees of humans in the garden of history.

There is father, proud, manly and looking very large,
In control, providing and very much in charge,
Family being the greatest institution in the world,
And mother, beautiful, shining like a black pearl.

Along came the children doing just what children do,
Eventually, growing into men and women starting life anew.
God's garden keeps on growing until it fills a great big field,
With so much love and humanity it has yield.

This big field has turned into a great big world,
All from the seed from a great black pearl,
And our family today is this wonderful union,
Who has gathered together in sweet communion.

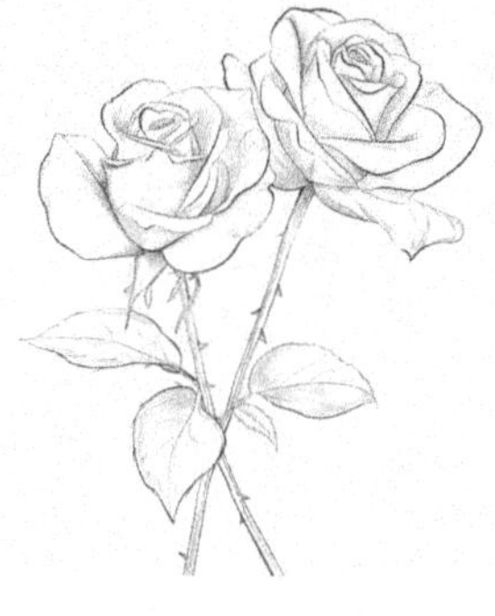

Vote for Wes

Hi folks it's me again,
With one more appeal for Wes.
I've watched his campaign over time,
For one He's better than the rest.
His warm and friendly manner is
as wide as a church's tall steeple.
He walks among, he reaches out and
puts hands on the people.
His background shows he's
capable of running this great state.
This beautiful state of Maryland,
along with his running mate.
This is his time and you can trust him,
united together we can help him win.
So, on election day leave your worries
behind, grab your coat, rally your
friends and neighbor and go Vote.

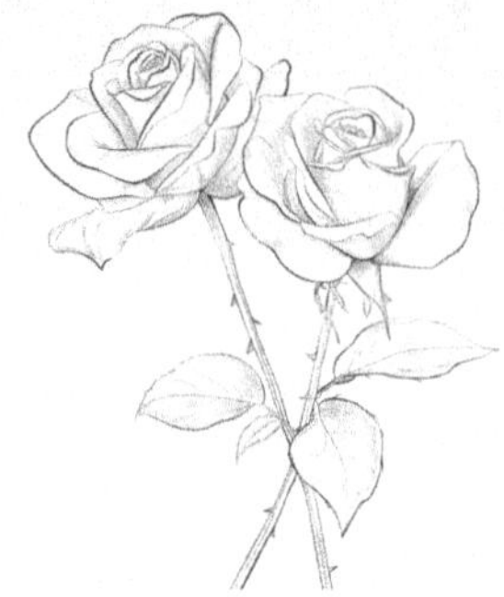

Newtown twenty boys

To the original twenty boys
And you know who you are
Your journey was a troubled one
But you each emerged a star

You all have had some trying times
Back in the day of twenty
But the thing that was so obvious
Was the love which was aplenty

You guys from a very young
Age all came together
You stayed strong throughout a
Lot of grief
Pulled thru troubles and whatever

No one can doubt the love you each had for the other
And to this day you treat one another as they were your
brother

Reaching out with a love that's strong
Staying together bringing each other along

Throughout sickness and trials of many kinds
Showing true value with love that binds

The community is a new one now with hope it will survive
If the young men show the kind of love that keeps the spirit
alive

So here's to the young men that is there today
May they be the kind of men who can stick it out and stay

to show the children and the families how to share in the
joys, like the community did back in the day of the original
twenty boys

CF

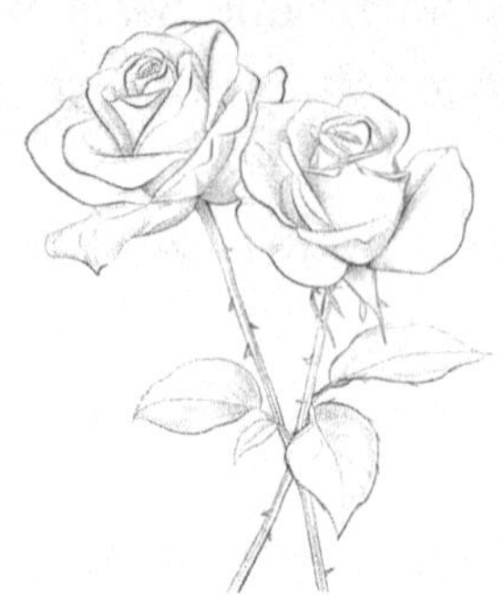

My Tribute to Lula Mae

Lillian Jeanette Butler, my friend Lula Mae,
We are here to celebrate you on this God given day.

While you, dear friend, have left us and gone on home to
glory, you did not leave without having left behind a story.

Having lived a long and wonderful life there is much you
have to tell, although it was filled with many storms, much of
it went quite well.

There was this loving family of yours to whom you gave
support, your sisters, brothers all the struggles you bared,
what a battle you must have fought.

Their children, your children all fared quite a feat, all
because you care so much and was so very sweet.

You kept them all together, endowed them with your love,
You instilled in them the love given you from a loving God
above.

You have now gone home to heaven in the sky.
You are not here now, but gave your loved ones time to say
goodbye.

The family kept a prayer vigil while you just slept to wait on
God to come and take you home thru the pearly gate.

Your soul mate Bo was there to great you and took you by
the hand, together now the two of you are at peace in God's
spiritual land.

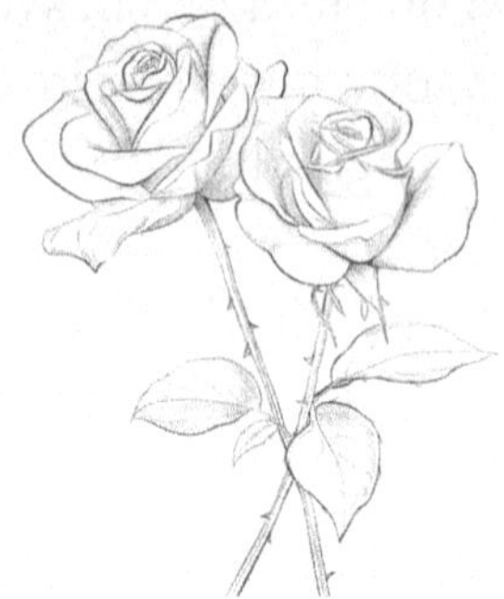

God's Gift of Love

This old world just ain't what it used to be,
And I'm sure it will never be the same,
Things have gotten out of control and
we wonder whose to blame.

People are different, they do things differently
And time has brought about a change,
One day its hot, the next day its cold,
Even the weather has become strange.

Are we getting the message
That's coming loud and clear,
Folks are doing their own thing and
Refusing to adhere,
To the commands of God that came
From above.
To go out in the world and share
His gift of Love

It's love that keeps this world intact
You can't go wrong, that's a fact

And while we see the things of the world
Have become so diverse,
God's love for mankind is still prevalent
Throughout the universe.

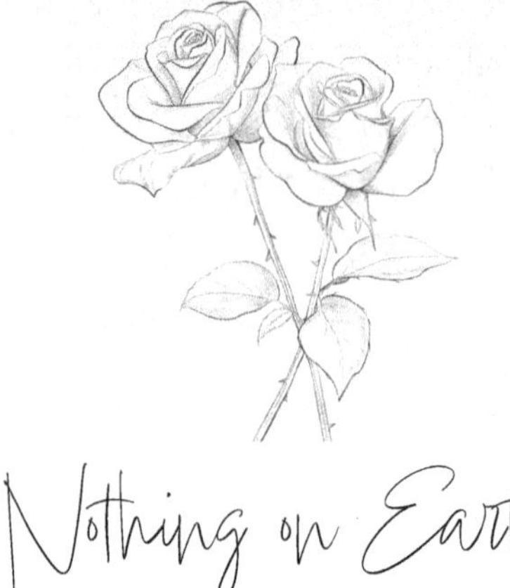

Nothing on Earth

There is nothing on earth like a friend,
Someone with you from beginning to end,
There is nothing on earth like a friend,
With whom you have had a time to spend,
To talk about the good times you have had,
As well as the times that were sad,
It's the good times that stays on your mind,
To remind you that life has been kind,
You treasure the moments you have spent,
And think about what it has all meant,
That through it all you were never alone,
For God, himself set the tone,
He followed your time here on earth,
From the moment, the very beginning of your birth,
Until now, till the end of your days,
Sent a friend who sticks with you and stays,
Who shows there is nothing on earth like a friend,
Who stays truly a friend to the end.

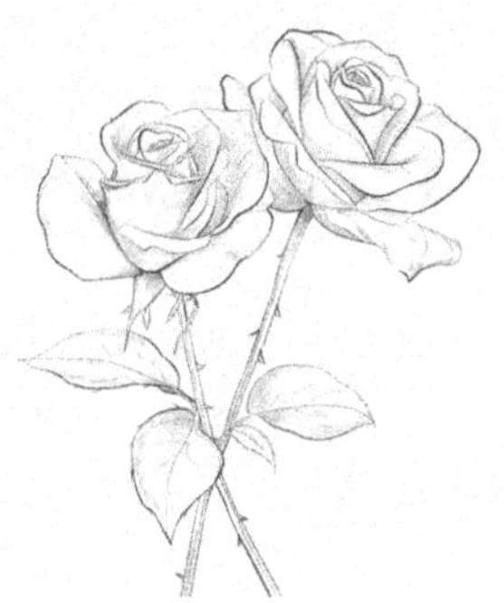

Women Working Together For Christ

Good morning, I am honored to be chosen as one of the women to speak to you today on the theme "Women Working Together for Christ."

I have chosen to speak the names of some of the Pioneer Women of First Baptist Church that I knew and remembered.

73

Women who were constantly working together for Christ, daily, weekly and constantly without ceasing. Whether it was cleaning the church, planting flowers, holding meetings, fundraising organizing and evangelizing it was all done for Christ.

Christ was born of a woman and God endowed women with love. Love of Christ, self, family and community.

Women who are mothers, grandmothers, aunts and sisters, sometimes moving in the midnite hour, coming to the aid of the lost and distressed. Listening to them, walking with them, leading them on the path to righteousness. Women working together for Christ.

These women were Sunday School teachers, ministry leaders, deaconesses or just Christian women moving the church forward.

So I just want to speak the names of these pioneer women who generations later still have women in the church working together for Christ.

Beginning with my own mother and Denise Smiths' grandmother Blanche McGowan, Annie Cruchfield- Carolyn Olds and Dous Betheas mother, Edith Lewis- Keeleys grandmother, Doris Turner- Deborah Hurley's mother, Edna Weems-, Dora Bundy- Julia Bowman, Elizabeth Watkins-, Louise Ford- Sadie Harris, Elizabeth Tyler- Myra's grandmother, Rosie Simms- Clytee's grandmother, Annie Johnson- Denise and Kim's grandmother, Sarah and Elaine Smothers, Mollie Harris, Maude Campbell, Ruth Thomas, Edith Gantt, Rebecca Thomas, Evelyn Morris, Sarah Perry, Rosil Taylor, Adele Walker, Ethel Thompson, Mary C. Brown,

I could go on and on naming pioneer women all working together for Christ, but I will end with this poem written for today.

Women Working Together for Christ

Women working together for Christ are like precious gems, Bright and beautiful, like flowers on long stems.

Women singing, praying for all whom they hold dear, Remembering their loved ones far and near.

Smiling women comforting, holding a hand,
Being a friend, taking a stand.

Women working together for Christ have much to be proud,
For the praises given God, constant and loud.

Women working together for Christ have all taken a vow,
To hold true to the values of Christ somehow.

Thanks to all women here today,
That's working together for Christ and leading the way.

75

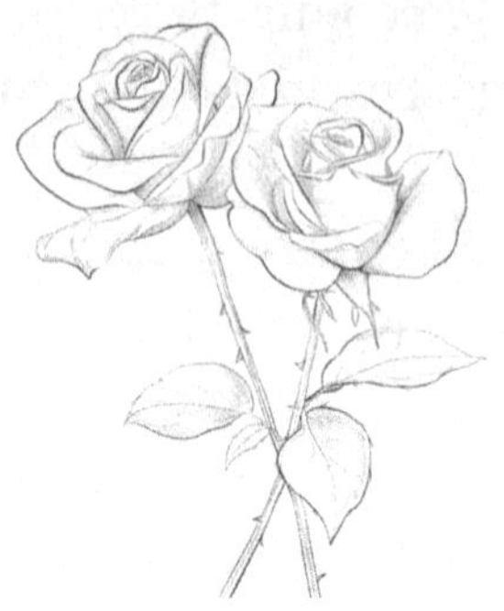

Marching In the Street

Here we go, here we go, here we go again,
Marching in the street for our brother who was slain,
Killed by the police who kneed on his neck
It's happening all too often, please
Give us a break
Black lives matter just as white lives too,
God made all lives,
Not just me and you
Men must come together, justice must prevail,
Until it does we all will suffer harsh winds, wild fires and
hail,
Brothers killed by police must come to a stand still,
Or God's fury will reign down and purge the earth if He will,
Mankind is made by God and is not man's to destroy
This universe and all within was made for God's own joy,
As the saying goes "Watch out brother how you walk on the
cross, your foot might slip and your soul get lost."

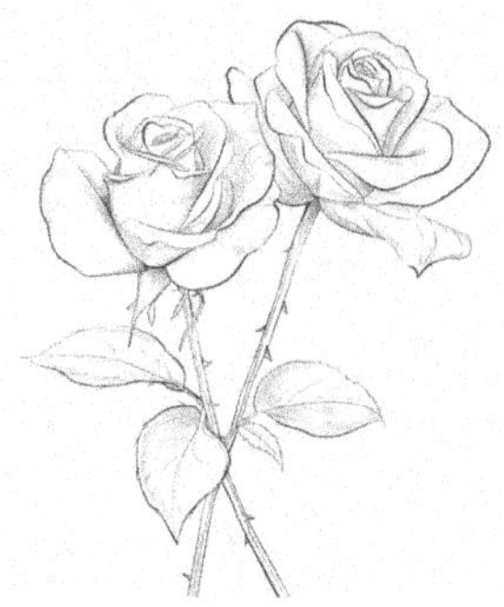

From Boys to Men

From boys to young men to men you must go.
It's time to stop playing and start acting the pro.
No more cowardly pranks like shooting at groups.
These are your people and part of the troops.
You are connected to those families somehow down the
line,
So you are wiping out kinfolks, yours and mine.
God didn't create you to harbor such hate.
You were created to love, that was your fate.
But you let Satan in to mess up your mind,
Whose soul interest is to control you and your kind.
So, turn back to your creator and confess your sin,
He will forgive you and take you back in.
He will love and protect you and you must do the same,
For your people from now on in Jesus' name.

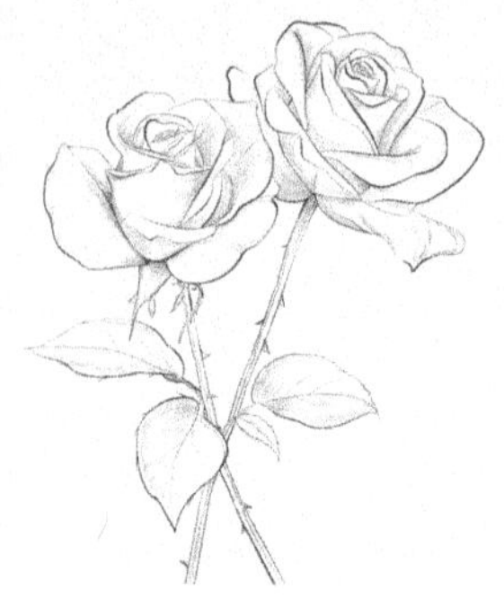

In Remembrance of Jeffrey

I'll remember Jeff, a great friend, a gentleman and a gentle man,
Quiet, well poised who traveled frequently to his ancestors land

He was interested in learning about his African background,
He went to Egypt where his history was found.

His journey took him well over twenty years,
Some of what he learned cost him a lot of tears.

As a people he learned we had lost much,
But, he was glad that he reached back and made the touch.

His people were first in this God given nation
And thanks to God made quite a sensation.

He learned that he was a man from kings,
And we, as a people were first inventors of many things.

He is still traveling, but in a better land,
He'll be remembered as the great historian.

Jeff has gone on to a new beginning,
This is not his end,
So, fare thee well Jeff,
You've been a good friend.

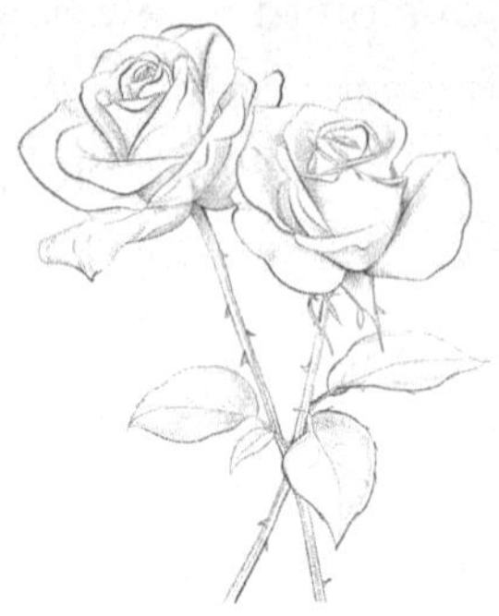

Going to the Promised Land

Good morning church, Wow! What a wonderful sight,
Look at the women of God all dressed in white.
They have been marching up and down praying and singing,
moving all about greeting and mingling.
In God's house just having a ball,
Watching, waiting for God to call.
We know He is coming, we just don't know when,
He has come for some, how long has it been.
Since they struck up the band,
and marched gloriously to the Promised Land.
When it's my turn to go to the promised land,
Jesus will come and take my hand.
He'll lead me up to the gate that is opened wide,
I will be free to step inside.
Waiting to greet me are my mom and dad,
I'll be so happy and oh so glad.
To see my brothers and sisters who are there too,
They will hug me and say we were waiting for you.
Your children and family members are just waiting around,
gathering together while you touch holy ground.

What a happy day and glorious jubilee,
all of us connecting to the family tree,
That was planted by Jesus eons ago
bearing good fruit while it was below.
It's back now on holy ground,
Back to it's beginning where it was first found.
And so here we are at our journeys end,
Where with the rest of our days with Jesus we'll spend.
We'll turn out in white just as we did today.
Thanks to Jesus, we are on our way.

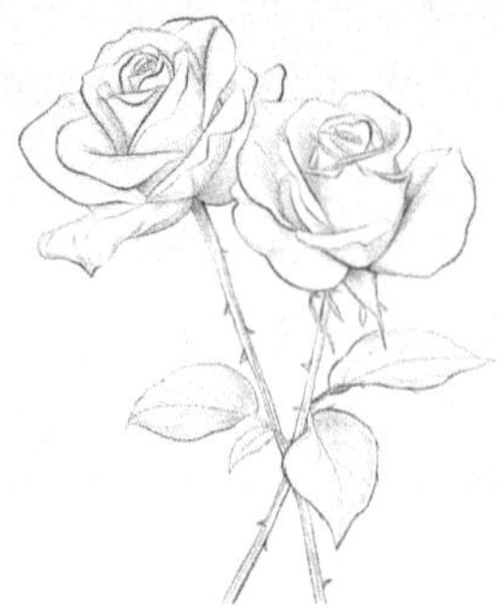

The Call to Women

Calling all women young and old
This is the story as it was told
God's harvest is a plenty, but the laborers are few
There is work for everyone, me and you
Come now to Jesus, work, serve in his vineyard, don't wait
Don't say you'll come tomorrow because tomorrow
may be too late
There is a mission for God's women as well as God's men,
Come alone if you have to, men will come
when God says when
He is speaking to you today, work is good for soul
There are arms waiting to greet you, come in and
join the fold
Work, for the day is coming when man will work no more
Come, work, receive your reward in God's heavenly store.

82

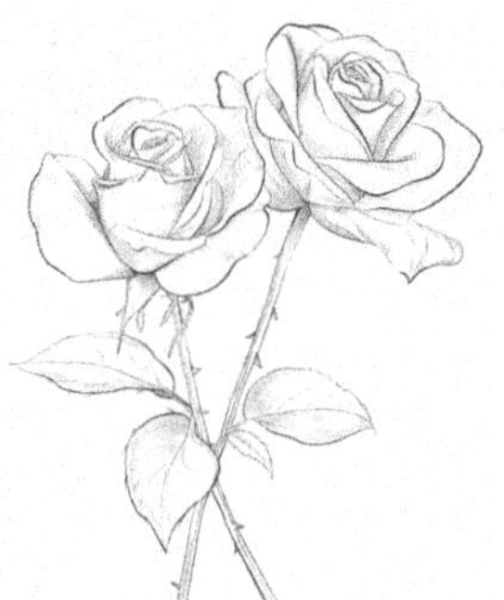

First Baptist Church of Annapolis

First Baptist Church of Annapolis
A solid church on a solid rock,
Whose pews are filled with God's special stock,
From a church in the woods we have come afar,
Traveling in time, following God's star,
Standing of the promises of God for 130 years,
Overcoming many trials and many tears,
God is still with us and has kept us strong and true,
Constantly keeping watch on everyone of you,
He is faithful with his justice, his kindness, and goodwill,
Knowing we are not perfect, He loves us still,
For 130 years the church has blessed this town,
Because of God's grace the church was kept around,
Thank you God for your trust,
Thank you God for choosing us,
It's been 130 years and God has been great,
So choose God today, tomorrow may be too late,
The ship is turning everyday,
And we must sincerely submit or lose our way.

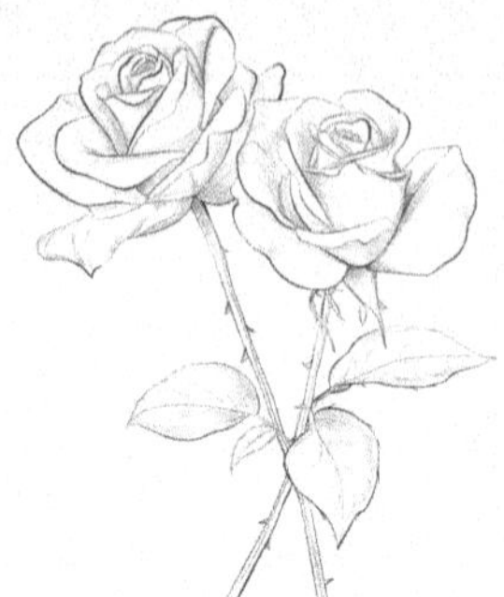

Delegate Sheneka Henson

Delegate Sheneka Henson, the delegate for district thirty,
She was chosen by the people who knew she was worthy.

She is the best delegate in the state,
Her constituents love her at any rate,
She is our own hometown girl,
A gem of a women, another real live pearl.

She care about her district,
And looks out for her folks,
Keeps them up to date on happenings,
And that's no joke.

When it comes to folks in Maryland
And that's her state,
She jumps right in with good ideas,
That determine Maryland's fate.

This is not just another politicians yarn,
Sheneka does her homework, she cares and gives a darn.
We need to remember her, keep her name in mind
Make sure she stays in office when it comes to voting time.

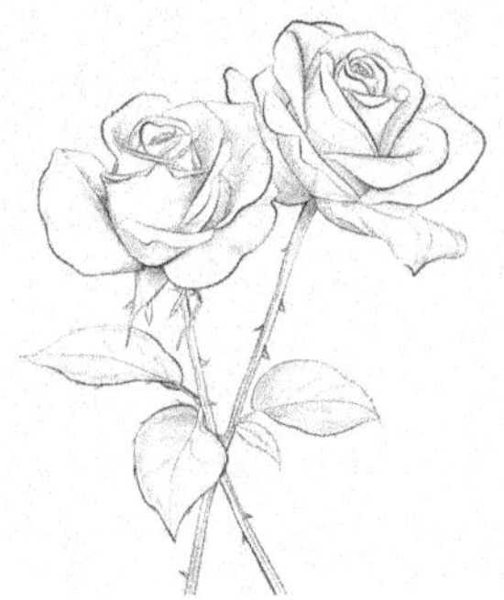

Cheers to Sheriff Sesker

Hear ye, Hear ye everyone and all,
Folks of renown,
You all know by now there's a new sheriff in town.
He's from the old fourth ward,
Does not play any tricks,
You know his mom of course is our own Penny Hicks.
He served law enforcement well over eight years.
He's strong, mighty, brilliant and honest.
Well respected by his peers.
He will protect us from all villains and save for us our day.
So here's three cheers for
Sheriff Sesker
Hip, Hip, Hooray

85

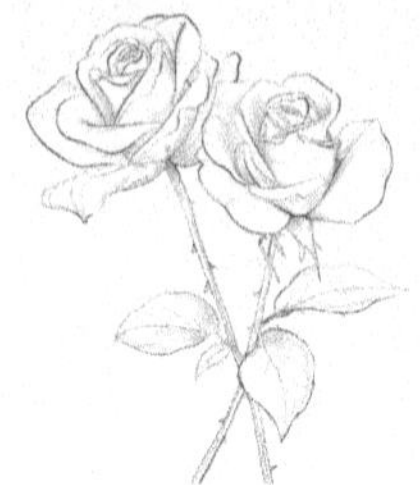

Wes' First Year as Governor

Hip, Hip, Hooray, three cheers for Wes,
For his first year in office, he passed the test.

He kept his promises and Gave so much more,
He listened to the citizens For whom he opened the door.

Our Lieutenant Governor, Aruna Miller, is also in the mix;
She has his back. Stays on his side, Together they plan and fix.

He has proven his love for our Maryland, the land we all love,
Thank you, sweet Jesus, looking down from above.

And God keep him humble and honest and true,
Keep him safe from all harm. And worthy of you.

Let him continue as governor and continue to lead,
Because he is your child, he will continue to succeed.

And Wes, he is so needed and loved by most.
We want him to continue as Maryland's host.

And God, thank you so much for paving the way for Wes,
For Maryland and America today.

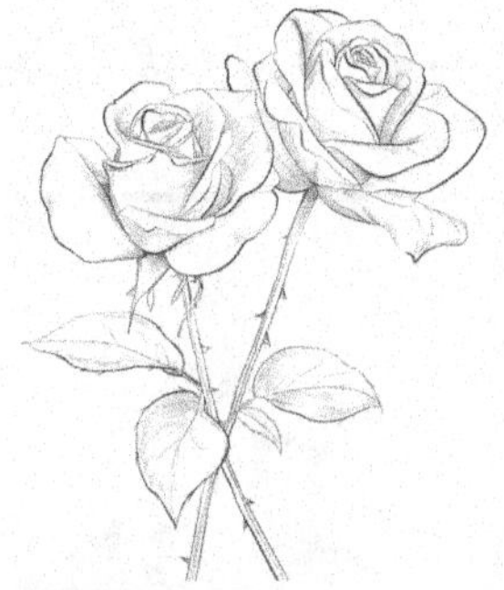

Pastor Wainwright

We were looking for a new pastor here at
First Baptist Church.
The pulpit committee got together
and started to pursue their search.
They interviewed and met with many Pastors from a source,
Choosing several after meeting, they finally had a choice.
The congregation got their chance
to hear them preach at last.
And when it came time their vote they did cast.
You, Pastor Wainwright, were by far the greatest one,
The congregation chose after all the voting was done.
So, to our new Pastor, Welcome,
and a hearty how do you do.
Words cannot express how happy we are to greet you.
Not forgetting God who was with us all the way.
Thanks to Him, and you and everyone
on this Installation Day!

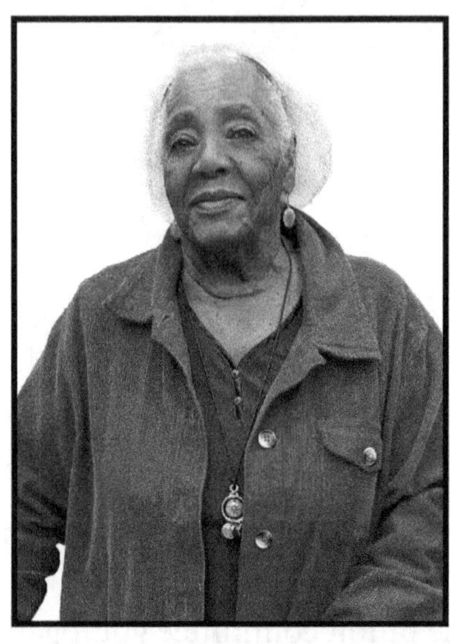

Elizamae Robinson is a native Annapolitan and a member of the First Baptist Church of Annapolis. A tireless advocate for the poor, she has dedicated her life to helping people.

A mother and grandmother, her forte is working with people regardless of race, age, gender, or political ideology. She has received numerous awards for her civic participation.

Mrs. Robinson, who helped organize the longest rent strike in the City of Annapolis, was also appointed by former Mayor Josh Cohen to the Housing Authority for the City of Annapolis.

She is a published author, and her book "Elizamae Robinson Speaking Poetically" is a collection of poems, including one about the first Maryland African American governor, Governor Wes Moore.

www.ingramcontent.com/pod-product-compliance
Lightning Source LLC
Chambersburg PA
CBHW061038050726
47592CB00004B/1496